I WANT MY COUNTRY BACK

BRUCE L. ETTER

ISBN: 1453677992
ISBN-13: 9781453677995

Printed by CreateSpace
7290-B Investment Drive
North Charleston, SC 29418
www.CreateSpace.com

Cover Design by Bruce L. Etter

DEDICATION AND ACKNOWLEDGMENTS

To everyone who has touched my life and enabled me to see the beauty in every breath I take. From my first day as a newborn to the present, I have been blessed by countless people including family, friends, fellow citizens, and foes—all have guided me along this pilgrimage called life, and I have become a truer spirit having crossed their path.

May the contribution they have made to my life be reflected in the grace with which I write about our continuing heritage as a people and my longing to bequeath a legacy that enables those who follow to promote the will that bonds and delivers us all, not only as citizens of the greatest nation on earth but as stewards to a world without end. May all your hearts run deep with passion, may all your visions come to glory, may the discipline of everyday life bring you comfort, and may the spirit that gives you life connect us all to a higher cause.

I especially want to dedicate this book:

To my loving wife, Mariellen, and adoring children, Greg and Lauren, for their unending patience and unwavering support without which this book would never have come to fruition. They have tolerated my many moods and tiring rhetoric while I have aspired to convey—in the following pages—my views, prayers, and wishes for a better country than the one we inherited from our parents.

Also, to my mother and father who early on planted the seeds of real value in my life, teaching and instilling in me the true measures of success and character.

To my brothers, Miles, Mike, Glenn, and their families who over the years have inspired me to follow my passions by pursuing their own.

To my Uncle Wynn, whose zest for life through good times and bad has taught me to live each day to its fullest.

To my in-laws Ann and Walt, whose love truly knows no bounds.

To my departed sisters, Patty and Sue, whose courage to live through pain and carry their faith into eternity has shown me a greater purpose in life.

To my sister, Nancy, and brother, Gene, who personify the meaning of "It is better to give than receive"!

And to our family dog, Beckham, for his unconditional love.

Finally, to the Delran United Girls soccer team, which I coached, for continually inquiring as to how my book is going and when am I going to have it published.

TABLE OF CONTENTS

Preface vii

Introduction xvii

1. Where We Stand.. 1

2. Human Rights: The Lack of Morality............................7

3. The Rich and the Poor: No In-between 11

4. Education, a Privilege or a Right? 17

5. The Disregard for Our Environment 25

6. Medical Advance and Its Limited Allocation 33

7. Propping up the Economy on Big Business While
   Main Street Falls Apart 39

8. Illegal Immigration and the Sweatshop Mentality That
   Both Bankrupts and Fuels Its Illegality........................ 47

9. America's Addictions to Drugs (Legal and Illegal)........... 53

10. Our Love Affair with Escaping Reality........................ 59

11. How Materialism and Capitalism Have Consumed the
    Core Values of Democracy...................................... 65

12. Our Paradise at the Expense of the World, and Who
    Will Pay for It... 71

13. Righting a Listing Ship.. 77

14. Draft for Community Service................................... 83

15. Nationalizing and Regulating Essential Vital Industries
    That Service All Americans 87

16. Re-gentrifying America: Building Tomorrow's Industries
    around Solving Today's Problems 93

17. Fighting Terrorism with Education and Nonviolence.......103
18. Challenging Today's Youth to Dream and Envision a
    Better Tomorrow 109
Epilogue...115
References 121
Notes 123

PREFACE

    We are the generation our parents labeled baby boomers, that was gifted so much and has held out so little in terms of bequeathing tomorrow's nation promise, hope, vision, and adventure. We don't even attempt to covet our most precious asset—an educated future with values that garner us rights to pursue life liberty and happiness.

    By "rights," we mean both freedom and responsibility. We've been blessed in our life time with an abundance of just about everything imaginable, yet we've managed to erode the roots that have given us the ability to reap so much—we've forgotten how to sow! In the race and quest of our generation to become the wealthiest, fastest, and all-encompassing democracy, we have forgotten about the blood, sweat, and tears it took to afford us our opportunity to play out our dreams. We've become an uneducated society that is consumed in our own wants, desires, and greed rather than filled with grace, gratitude, and the passion to extend our good fortunes into brighter caring opportunity for tomorrow's world. We have condoned apathy, ignorance, and blissfulness to create the stench called mediocrity that we wallow in today. To have it better than the past is now only measured and quantified in material terms; the real, intangible wealth that fueled the engine for our growth has sadly been replaced by the spinning wheel of power and self-satisfaction. We are like a modern-day Roman Empire that keeps on playing the violin as it fades into the unquenchable fires of extinction.

The ransom we have kidnapped our children's future for can only be satisfied by us. We need to collectively assess and evaluate that the pain it takes to continue along this self-destructive, numbing journey is far greater than the sacrifices we must presently make to change tomorrow into a course of faith, hope, and vision. We must brush the dust off the intangible fabric that truly defines success and once again build unity, trust, and openness in this ever-diverse land we live in.

Without educating and tooling this country's men and women of tomorrow, we deplete our most precious asset and leave them not only defenseless to our adversaries but stripped of the ability to take on the real challenges that confront this nation and the world at large. Without conveying knowledge and inciting provocative thought, we not only loose tomorrow, we lose the present and the past.

As the major super power of the twentieth and twenty-first century, we are driving the course of humankind right out of existence. We have ceased acting with the intention to elevate humankind from within and, in fact, have regressed to a form of social Darwinism that reacts to every fire with a match. We can only hold out hope to our children by facing our own fears and shortcomings, and risk losing the comfort of today so that the warmth we once knew can abound again tomorrow. We must take a reality check of the situation we now live in and sincerely form and implement positive proactive plans with our own blood, sweat, and tears that will foster lasting solutions to today's problems, as well as spawn new sense of purpose in tomorrow's world.

We now have to confront our biggest nemesis, greed, and all its constant lust for power; change the course of the game; and change the way we participate in it. We can no longer neglect our responsibilities to each other and our successors in the quest for the almighty greenback. Not only to survive but to flourish we must live a lifestyle the rest of the world respects and is willing to relate with. We must see our neighbors and ourselves as we really are and parley our diversity into strengths that afford us the ability to transcend the limits of our past into a peaceful, bountiful world of the future. We must make our new vision open and beneficial to all by making everyone beneficial to humankind. We must spell it out and make it clear that in order for all of us to perpetuate life; we have to become educated to the gifts and talents we can bring to the table. We must cast aside the negatives that each and every one of us continually harbor and instead promote the positive attributes that naturally bring out our best and provoke others to do likewise.

We must preserve our roots in order to grow and shape the tree. Under all is still the land that was left to We the People, so it is up to US citizens to live and change the core values of our society. Values we as a nation were born from, wish to be part of, and want to pass on to future generations.

History, as it always has, will expose the truth, and with the truth we will be set free to chart our course. Spin it, market it, promote it any way you wish; through the eyes of Father Time history is written, and through eternal eyes history has been made flesh. "The stakes are high and the time is now to become the change we long to see."[i] The road to a better tomorrow has to have vision and be crafted with a passionate commitment that manifests today's issues and turns them into tomorrow's cornerstones. We must start to address and resolve what's been festering in our own hearts, minds, bodies, and souls so that moving forward we positively impact the good of our society.

For far too long we have lain dormant, only taking action when we can obtain a significant part of what's to be gained. We as a nation are being pressured with change both internally and externally. The question being put before every one of us in our daily living is whether or not we have the intestinal fortitude to act with grace under pressure. Are we willing to put the needs of others in front of our own needs, wants, and desires? And are we willing to part with greed and self-gratification in order to afford our brother the same opportunities with which we've been gifted? Can our generation go the extra mile so that future generations can afford to dream anew and experience life through the eyes of a child once more—innocent and in awe of the pilgrimage they will embark upon while entrusted and confident with knowing they've been passed a solvent path to journey from?

We must dream, design, test, and develop with focus, clarity, commitment, flexibility, and realism that parallel the intensity our forefathers displayed when they revolutionized this great land. Our challenges hold as much if not more risk than what they were faced with, and yet the opportunities to again enrich and pass on to the future ring as loud as the Liberty Bell did when it ushered in our freedom back in 1776.

As we delve into the second decade of the twenty-first century, we find ourselves standing in the crossroads of what we once were and stood for and how we are looked upon today by each other and the world at large. Change is ever eminent, and the actions we take to procure these changes will have a lasting effect on where we stand as a sovereign state. How we relate to our fellow citizens and how we are valued in the world of tomorrow will depend on how "united" we become going forward. In order to bring about change, we must first address the reality of where we are at present in terms of the values we hold ourselves accountable to and the democracy we try to live and represent.

Since the beginning of the new millennium, we've become a polarized nation that stands divided on every main issue brought to the forefront of our times. As a society we sit back and wait apathetically for our "leaders" to come up with resolve and direct this nation to a clearer course. Reality shows that politics in this country on all levels have become as bad as professional sports with regard to serving the people. The political arena has boiled down to self-serving pundits who, with their war chest of money, pacify enough of their constituency to get elected then spend their time in office trying to stay elected rather than committing to serving the population they've been elected to represent. How many times over the past decade have we seen and accepted the negative mudslinging campaign advertisements that don't even begin to address the real issues or hold out promise for positive growth and change. Instead, all we get from the candidates is wasted time, resources, and a failure to plan for the future. If candidates spend all their resources and effort in this kind of negative campaigning, then why are we so surprised when they get elected that nothing positive and visionary gets implemented for the good of the people?

Modern-day politics has become just the opposite of what democratic governing is supposed to be: public service. It has become a bastion for self-serving people who mask themselves as either Democrat or Republican but really only hold allegiance to the opportunistic agenda that they and their backers have negotiated long before they hit the campaign trail. Wouldn't it be refreshing and revolutionizing in this day and age to have some true public service–minded people come forward—people who work for the good of the public and benefit by serving those they have been elected to represent—and take on these powers to be for the good of the people? In order to bring about this type of change, we need to ask ourselves some basic fundamental questions and educate ourselves to the real facts.

We must use the six honest serving men who taught us all we knew; where, what, when, how, why, and who. By educating ourselves to the issues of the day and where our representatives' stand on these matters, we can constructively make decisions and act responsibly for our causes with the hope and faith that when everyone is doing their part to support this democracy, positive results will take hold.

Democracy is an active process whereby everyone who lives under it has an obligation to take part in it. Whether we are running for office or being represented by the office, we all have the duty to be informed and vote our conscience. Once representatives are elected, we have the new responsibility to stay tuned to what they say and do on our behalf, and in doing so give feedback to those who represent us.

You see, freedom has its responsibilities, and being free in a democratic society spawns a relationship between those who govern and those being governed. Just as in personal relationships, in order to grow and mature, daily nurturing by all parties involved needs to be provided. A give-and-take, learn-as-we-go, all-in-this-together type mentality has to blossom for a culture such as this to mature and develop. By relating with those who serve us, we can truly be free to pursue interests and concerns that affect our daily living and affect how we are looked upon from the outside world. We may not see eye-to-eye on every topic that our elected officials are challenged with, but if we openly dialogue with and relate to these matters at hand we can rest assured that our representatives will have every point of view from which to choose what's best for the good of the whole. The more input We the People provide to our representatives, the better prepared these officials will be to decide what's best for the community. In true democracy, the people really do govern themselves; so to become apathetic and only educate ourselves to surface propaganda and take into account only what benefits our individual selves today is to shortchange the lasting benefits our government has been set up to accomplish.

We the People must first be accountable to ourselves and each other by contributing as much to the process as we can; then we must hold those who serve us accountable for the actions they take on our behalf. The beauty of our democracy lies in the way our forefathers formed it (executive, legislative, and judicial): a government that forms checks and balances to account for its actions and ensure that it is working for all the people.

The reality of where we stand today is that We the People as a whole have failed to live up to our responsibilities. With our passive, apathetic, and ignorant approach to caring for our freedom, we have let those who wish to exploit the system for their own personal gain. Democracy is not a system of handouts and giveaways, where Big Brother will lead you by the hand. We as citizens of this great experiment must continually educate ourselves to the facts and must actively participate in the shaping of its growth. We must actively enact our rights to hold those who represent us and our concerns to the fire of fulfilling the duties we have entrusted them with. This means those who are willing to serve us should be accountable to us for the ways in which they do in fact serve.

We can't just sit back and expect our government to automatically do what's best for us; we must continuously be active, knowledgeable participants in our own governing. This entails getting the facts and voting your conscience based on your assessment of the raised concerns. Today more than ever the responsibility of freedom rests on the shoulders of We the People; if we don't educate ourselves to the issues that are shaping our tomorrow and don't raise our voices through casting our votes, then we only have ourselves to blame when the outcome of our apathy leads us to insurmountable challenges and suffocates any opportunity for growth.

We stand where we are today because we have allowed the situation to evolve without fulfilling our rights to become active participants in the process. We rationalize away our inactive positions by saying that one person cannot make a difference. In fact, it is because one-by-one our forefathers stood up to the predicament of the day and chose to actively be heard and establish rights for individuals that we have a country 230 years later with the world democracy and true freedom to bring about change—change that affects us, and We the People are the ones who determine whether that change is beneficial or undermining.

We see great unrest and much division in our society today, both domestically and in our foreign affairs, because we have been way too busy hurling daggers at our neighbors in defending our own interests rather than sharing the benefits of what we have earned in the hopes of enriching everyone's plight. We have insulated ourselves from reality to the point where once reality starts to hit home, we react with a defensive, removed posture, ignoring the fact that our own perception and inactivity have led us to the present day situation. Or we've become so protective of our view of reality that when the truth actually confronts us, we cease to be open to it. This leads to rift and divide and opens the floodgates of negativity, depression, and hopelessness. In this environment we don't even have time to stop and enjoy the fruits of our labor; we can't see the leverage to be gained by embracing our diversity, in turn opening up new paths and byways to overcome today's struggles and roadblocks.

As we move into the twenty-first century and our political system remains gridlocked in a neglected, divided vision of how we can live united in tomorrow's world, we must also reflect on how we perceive technology and the Information Age to carry us to a brighter dawn. Since the beginning of the information and technology boom, we have constantly been striving for bigger, faster, more elaborate, and more automated ways to enhance our lifestyles. But in the process of reaching this utopia we have diminished and dehumanized the very environment in which we live. We have replaced living for each other and the betterment of the whole with satisfying our individual comforts and entertaining our own wants. Going for the brass ring has become an obsessive sport in which the cost to our neighbor, the environment, and our future are outweighed by the greed of experiencing self-satisfaction and instant gratification in climbing to the top. We have lost sight of developing and enriching life in order to become rich, powerful, and famous. The price we pay for this high is often rationalized away by using a limited universe of information that statistically markets the benefits of our actions and dismisses carnage that is left in its wake. We must reinforce the positive attributes technology and information can have on us in solving inadequacies of today, and at the same time respect the human value to which we apply it to.

INTRODUCTION

For too long We the People of this great nation have stood idle, bellowing hot air at the multitude of issues and challenges that have been mounting within the confines of our country. Over the past ten years the administrations as well as our leadership have failed to invoke the fundamental services that the Declaration and Constitution obligate them to uphold.

But in the course of their failure we have been blinded to the responsibility of our own citizenship to be a check and balance for those who have been elected to serve for the whole. We have rationalized away our apathy in the old cliché: we can't fight city hall. We stand on the sidelines ranting and raving that politicians are nothing but self-serving pundits who run and get elected to satisfy their own wants and objectives. We accept the repeated route taken by candidates to run on image, spin, negativity, and a lack of vision or substance. We look for the kinks in everyone's armor instead of the hope and faith that some candidates believe they will and can make a difference for our society. We don't seek out truth and reality as much anymore because it is easier to look for comfort and self-gratification rather than sacrifice for a vision of a better tomorrow. We have become consumed in our own inequities to the point that even when we feel we are making headway; we are only really wallowing in our mediocrity.

On top of an inept leadership directing an uneducated; deluded society, we have managed to view the media as a demigod whose ambition is not to be factual but to produce profit on instant expertise without much fortitude in committing to truth and reality. Most of today's news is based on getting it first and getting it fast, not on getting the facts and getting it right. This leads us to being manipulated and coerced into a false reality, one that is the dominion of a few at the expense of many.

Today's media lacks sincere, honest investigative journalism that doesn't influence a defined outcome but rather seeks and searches for truth, justice, liberty, and discloses the facts—documenting history instead of fabricating it.

With all that said, I sincerely believe that as a people we can still mobilize and generate a better way of life not just for ourselves but for our neighbors and our future—if we will only take the time to foster a true vision that demands sacrifice, commitment, perseverance, flexibility, conscience, and the realization that life is cyclical and will not always progress forward in a linear fashion, that one step back is sometimes preferred in order to advance two steps forward, that humility can be regarded as strength and surrendering can lead to great faith and the ability to live free while helping others achieve their dreams. We can mutually benefit if we take the time to understand and foster one another. This takes an extreme amount of patience and education to leverage the diversity of one another for the good of all.

In order to make a better life for tomorrow, we must live each moment in the present and replace our own selfish wants with what will benefit the community. At the same time we must seek to expand the community to include those who hold the same core values yet may approach living from a different perspective. By continually developing and maturing an attitude that pushes our limitations of today in search of a brighter tomorrow, we start to expand our horizon and capture a bigger piece of the truth. To work, live, laugh, and love encompassing the notion that the more we experience—the more we realize there is to experience—the more we take on a new, promising dimension that opens up avenues to deal with the here and now, presenting a brighter, more confident future: one that re-crystallizes the American dream we were taught through the founding of our heritage.

We are not a pure people whose pedigree stature puts us above the rest of humankind. Rather we are a melting pot, a diversified lot who have been gifted a freedom to recognize we aren't perfect, nor are we uniform. It is out of unity striving for a better way of life for all that we can create a shining new vision that's based on the foundation of our past and will reside in a better tomorrow. We must all compassionately start living with one another to make life fulfilling for everyone and not at the expense of each another. We must stay focused on lessons learned and continually forge change in order to present the world that we seek.

We as Americans must live with the courage to make a difference, accept the challenges that come our way, and act with wisdom and the principles that make us who we are. God granted our forefathers the faith, courage, serenity, and wisdom to establish a nation that includes diversity, acceptance, unity, hope, and bounty—not to be hoarded like all the previous vanquished civilizations but to be shared by all her people as well as with the rest of the world. One nation under God should exemplify the service of God through caring for its people and sharing with the rest of the world: an opportunity to be responsible to one another while enjoying the freedom to pursue Life, Liberty, and Happiness.

We must reeducate ourselves as to where we have come from and how blessed we are to live where we do in the company of others seeking similar happiness and fostering visions, adventures that raise the level of all humanity to the place where God initially created us to be. We are, as humans, a gift from God to God for all the inhabitants of this planet to marvel. We were made to keep stewardship over a piece of heaven so filled with splendor and awe that it continually takes one's breath away. Our forefathers in their varying degrees took notice of this fact and, instead of submitting to the tyranny of a king who had been corrupted by power and the illusion that his ideals and contents were the end all, took action through faith to lead us into a land that would embrace freedom, liberty, and justice of all rather than just the privileged few. They visualized outside their mortal existence to form a United States that would afford all her citizens the rights and responsibilities to tenure and steward the greatest bounty gifted to us; further, to perpetuate the dream that humans could emulate their Creator in the spirit with which God created us.

We all have talents and skills which, fueled by passion and understanding, will lead us to the success we were born to live. By serving others and honoring our community, we learn to "ignite the passion of our hearts, which in turn drives the vision of our minds and motivates the discipline of our actions while obeying our consciences that reign with the spirit breathed into us to manifest for the greater good of humanity."ii We realize that our existence has been preordained and that our being is limited by our mortality as it is witnessed in the present world. May the truth be told and, recognizing a promise for a better tomorrow—fruitful for eternity—lay waiting at our final slumber and make our quest here on earth to live, laugh, and love all that much more strongly, daring "to live each day as if it were our last."[iii]

To encompass the vision our God and this nation bestow on us, we need to tender to our brothers and sisters, humble ourselves to the gifts we can share, and enable our riches to mutually benefit those we share faith with in addition to those who oppose us yet hold the same flame deep in the recesses of their hearts. We are all in this together, and if we can be found, then we can find those who have become lost. We must seek to make this journey a better ride and give insight to our neighbor by lighting the way.

America has always stood for what is shining and good and endearing. We have always been enamored with the rest of the world and have displayed an intrinsic value to lead by serving—our truly great leaders who have embraced our heritage then added value to it—by gifting back what has been gifted to us, by enabling others to pursue their freedom and liberty. All humanity has benefited from this potent resolve, and now in our present position within the world, we should reflect on and strengthen the values that have grown us as a nation, that have allowed us to defy extinction like past civilizations and have continually gentrified a people who from time to time have suffered from selfish, neglectful, short-sighted transgressions—a people who only after surrendering to their own ineptitude have been willed the power to carry humankind to higher heights and afford more of its citizenry the ability to act on faith, hope, and love without fear of faltering or wilting to test and temptation.

Contrary to becoming finite a rising spirit to charge into the unknown in search of a new world is the underlying drive that keeps this American dream alive for those who seek to create a heaven here on earth. America is a gift to us; let us gift her back to the next generations with the openness that has kept her glowing for over 230 years. Let's take on the stewardship of preserving a nation under God, indivisible, with liberty and justice for all so that, looking down on her in the centuries to come, we can see a youthful society that lends its sovereignty, gifts, and talents to the world in order to make life better for all today, tomorrow, always. God bless the USA and spirit with which He has gifted her to us, "We the People," along with the ability to foster a better path for humanity.

Post Katrina New Orleans LA

WHERE WE STAND

1960:	2008:
USA Producer Nation	USA Services Consumer Nation
Camelot Era	Leaderless Era
Eisenhower Surplus Era	Biggest debtor Nation on the Planet
Energy robust Independent	Heavily Energy Dependent
Dollar backed by Gold Std	Dollar rapidly Declining
Strong Alliances in Europe	Weak Alliances due to Reckless Foreign Policy
Immigration welcomed	Immigration eroding us financially
Medical Care Open	Over 44 Million without Insurance
Education USA at Forefront	USA near the bottom
Virtually no Trade Deficit	Record High Trade Deficits
Civil Rights Major Concern	Equality still a Major concern
Concerns & Solutions Defined	Gray areas for issues & answers
Limited channels of distribution	Unlimited channels of distribution
Marketing preamble to substance	Marketing is the substance
Library cornerstone of Information	Internet provides unlimited resource
Life far more valued	Life exploited without empathy
Democracy in hands of people	Democracy limited to special interests
Core family unit married w/kids	Family unit all across the board

Prayer in Public Schools	Prayer forbidden in schools
Americans open & forthright with one another, felt unified with freedom as their mantra	Americans apathetic to national cause more concerned with escaping than living united
Dialogue done face to face	Dialogue virtual thru computer & texting
Human values intangibles were the glue that held this country together; causes were sought after with commitment & passion	Human value is distant & disconnected from material wealth& self gratification
The rule was the norm	The exception is the norm
More in tune to where we came from and where our neighbors came from and less concerned with getting ahead while leaving others behind. The American Dream was that I could fulfill my vision & my neighbor could fulfill his as well. In other words there was always enough room at the top for those who persevered and earnestly achieved. Because the successful American Dream meant sharing the spoils of success with those who helped along the way as well as those less fortunate	We are more concerned with getting to the top; at the expense of others; and greedily hoarding our spoils. We currently tend to seize opportunities for ourselves yet we fail to present opportunities to others once we've "made it on our own".

As a nation we have failed miserably. Where our fathers' generation took the time to create avenues for our success while "making it," our generation of baby boomers seemed to get stuck on "me" and forgot about creating inroads for those who follow. Subsequently, our children and their children are left digging out from under, which narrows their scope of opportunity and leaves no light for them to work openly toward.

Yet they see the bounty of our generation and want to capture it for themselves at the expense of being cutthroat and selfish for their own resolve. And where do you think this leaves their children and the nation at large? We have planted our seedlings in shallow, subpar soil and left them exposed to all the elements, all so we can be comfortable while we are at the helm.

In one respect you can't blame today's youth for the attitude they have. They have been left to fight for survival in a culture that touts tangible wealth as the zenith to success. We have failed to cultivate a healthy tree that will continue to grow and produce an abundance of fruit. When we stop nurturing the way we were nurtured for the sake of our own gratification, we begin to lose out on eternity and, in turn, cut off the prospects of our offspring having the chance to grow up in the image of the one who has endowed us with everything. We become fallen angels in a fallen nation. It is important to assess how far we've come realistically, and it is critical to see in what direction we are steering the ship. At present, we have all fallen asleep at the bridge; if we continue along this path we will run aground or worse sink to the bottom of the ocean.

Fortunately, by assessing where we stand we have begun to face the predicament we currently reside in. To reflect back on how we were afforded the opportunity to achieve the prosperity we have. To alter our attitude in order to move forward in the present so that the repeated greed and gluttony pattern gets broken. To open up a thriving new American Dream for the youth of today and tomorrow. To supersede the hoarding selfishness that has overrun the orchard and decayed not only the trees but the soil for future harvesting. We are not that far removed from more prosperous times where the plight of the whole community factored in the success of the individual citizenry. The lessons fostered and learned during these times are valuable resources for planning and tackling the challenges we are confronted with today.

Enhanced by technology that covers exponential ground for generating dreams and visions of tomorrow, we must keep our focus on benefiting the populous rather than fragmenting for self gain. We need to step back, inventory our resources, and find avenues that will become most productive and beneficial in solving the majority of obstacles that weigh us down and zap our spirit. It is imperative we recognize that the value of integrating technology into our everyday existence is still predicated on the intangible pillars that form the foundation of our soul as a nation. To become highly productive, efficient, and successful through technological advances without encumbering love, faith, hope, liberty, justice, and happiness as the driving force for this outcome is the same as squandering resources just to satisfy an immediate want. There is no lasting benefit, and what was once thought everlasting quickly becomes perishable.

Instead of fruitlessly pounding "democracy" down the rest of the world's throats; we should work on restoring democracy and the American dream here at home. By opening up vision and resourcing our own ingenuity and spirit, we can once again open up that envied ribbon of highway to the skyway, making a liberating lifestyle enticing once more. Only, this time around our attitude will be wiser and more humbling; maybe we can focus on solutions not only to national challenges but to global opportunities in which we play an intricate part. In addition to exporting our culture via

Coke, McDonald's, entertainment, Internet, processing technology, etc., we can educate our minds enough to export solutions to world hunger, disease, energy and utility concerns, as well as environmental concerns, peace building and other service-related, infrastructure-enhancing concerns that will allow undeveloped parts of the world to shine and contribute to the betterment of humankind.

By taking care of our own we will afford the rest of the world a chance to take care of themselves; more importantly we can establish inroads and relationships peacefully that will benefit everyone who seeks to covenant the treasure of life. This does not happen overnight, and it doesn't just pop up onto a computer screen. We must pay a bit of retribution to the rest of the world for enduring our selfish and greedy past, and the only way to pay this price and become whole with the rest of humanity is to become whole and kind with ourselves as a nation first. Through strengthening our resolve to reconcile and become what we profess to the rest of the world, we stay true to our convictions and convey a sincere, open, proactive message to those we engage with. Our values once again foster a nurturing, educating, sharing attitude that is not controlling but supportive. We are not the freedom crusaders of the globe; but when freedom is witnessed to be strong at home and a sense of unity and community is emulated to the world, the job of promoting and expanding similar cultures becomes an unconscious effort. It is not the prime intent; rather it becomes a freedom of choice for those who wish to partake in it.

This vision and direction also lends to reaffirm alliances and strengthen ties with those who place the same values on humanity and our place in the world. Enemies and foes will always be seeking absolute autonomy and in their quest for omnipotent power will either consume themselves or come to the realization that compromising and conforming is how they can really achieve an everlasting presence in the world. The world started out peacefully, and we have been trying to circumvent that peace ever since we were gifted with the freedom to think, choose, and act on our own. But through the test of time, our Creator has endured and peace has been an eternal goal. Violence and war, on the other hand, may rule for brief periods in history; but they are never an eternal goal, and those who advocate this policy become old and ultimately yearn for peace.

Throughout all of civilization the end result each side is trying to acquire is to live in peace and build a peaceful kingdom. The divide lies in the philosophical and ideological differences that each culture relies on to drive them toward their goals. In the end even the most powerful in the world come face-to-face with mortality and must search their souls to see where their eternal relationships will land them.

It all comes back to living in the present and accounting for our tenure and stewardship while growing and relating to each other as a society. Our faith can be viewed through the reflections of how we treat our fellow human, for we were all born from our mother's womb and the miracle of life has been gifted to each and every one of us from our Creator. In turn, He works through all of us fostering His love and granting independence and freedom of choice to act according to our conscience. This land of manifest destiny has been gifted to us in the hope that we will steward it in a way that endows fertile promise for generations to come; by gifting back and cherishing our precious time at the helm we can once more make this land the shining star it was thought to be when the first inhabitants came upon it.

HUMAN RIGHTS: THE LACK OF MORALITY

When it comes to human rights, actions speak louder than words. In recent years we have fallen terribly short in this category. Most people try to feel better by throwing cash at issues in this category; we fail to take the time and effort to understand and then act on a situation where we can truly make a difference. If it is in our own backyard, we usually end up fortifying our own bunkers and leaving those being affected to fend for themselves.

How can we sit back and allow our fellow citizens to toil and struggle to create a better life without offering some kind of assistance, understanding, and empathy? Have we become so disconnected as a community, as a nation, that we forsake aiding others in order to protect the bubble of comfort we are currently blessed with? Does out of sight, out of mind really work when striving to create a beneficial community that longs to stay united as a nation? Without identifying and addressing the human rights needs of our own people, how can we tout to the rest of the world that they need to treat their people responsibly?

The United States has more non-war, non–natural disaster murders than any country in the world. This is just the violent aspect of our lack for human dignity as a nation. Factor in corporate greed and practicing medicine as a business instead of a human obligation, and you are starting to get the present picture of where we fail to respect and enact human rights with our own neighbors, let alone neighboring countries.

We fail to adjudicate proportionately the punishment with the crime; as a society – with our current judicial system – we entitle our most unruly criminals with more inalienable rights then we give the victims or the rest of our law abiding citizens. We subsidize correctional facilities with taxpayer dollars; wouldn't it be more civil to restrict these guilty parties' rights as citizens since they usurped their freedom when committing the crime? Don't these un-abiding citizens owe society recompense at their own peril before having their full citizenship restored?

As for those who show no remorse for their acts against society, maybe we should think about stripping their citizenship permanently and deporting them to a land that will deal with the nature of their behavior more suitably. Maybe we should make the deterrent factor more stringent - a person without a country - so that thinking and valuing life at large before acting to satisfy one's own greed will compel potential criminals to be conscious of the consequences to be born before they decide to act out rather than pleading for another chance after they've committed the foul action. A stronger deterrent becomes more civil and beneficial to the society and forms a healthier community, placing less undue burden on that society to rehabilitate, reconcile, and restore those members who freely break the law. Subsequently, we should also have these guilty parties pay for the expense incurred to re-establish their good standing in the community. One alternative for this might be to brandish their wages over a period of time as recompense for the investment made to make them a positive productive part of the community once more.

Compound this with the open morality of what we let our children be subject to (as far as values are concerned), and we don't see a clear line as to right and wrong anymore. We teach them to rationalize away why there are the haves and the have nots and not to take a stand that would jeopardize what they have acquired—even if it would better serve them and the community in the long run. We don't need to revert back to a black-and-white, homogenous, uniform society because in reality we've never been a nation founded on this principle; but we need to educate, respect, and leverage our diversity to reinforce higher principles with regard to human rights. We need to reflect a unity that can be reinforced by our society to benefit all of that society, a national unity. We need to start treating and serving one another as if we are manifesting opportunity for "we" instead of "I."

If we learn to recognize our fellow citizens as having the same fundamental rights and liberties as we have, we begin to accept the positive diversity we all bring to the community, and the community echoes responsible action towards human rights. The need for ultra technological security being imposed externally is replaced by "trust" and "fiduciary responsibility" to freely engage in beneficial activity that not only advances our individual selves but the entire community. We begin to generate a constructive, peaceful, plentiful society rather than a destructive, fragmented society.

Restoring awareness of human rights will spawn action and policy that reinforces bounty for all classes of people opening up vision and prosperity for many, while assisting those less fortunate. We as a nation prosper and emulate to the rest of humanity that, relating to our neighbors with wisdom, flexibility, openness, and empathy, long-term wealth and stability can be fostered and even transcended not only at home but about the world. Those who continue to disregard their neighbor for the sake of self gain—as history attests—will become imprisoned in their own obsession for power and control. Eventually, their temporary dominance over their neighbors will wither. Human rights, like faith, are an inherited freedom that entails responsibility in order to celebrate in the liberties that stewardship produces. If we ignore the obligations that coincide with the reward we run the risk of revolution and retribution from those we fail to include in our grace and mercy.

THE RICH AND THE POOR: NO IN-BETWEEN

෨෩

The sad reality of our society today lies in the fact that we have created a culture that puts material wealth ahead of character, integrity, responsibility, understanding, and empathy towards our communities. America as we know it today has split into two classes—the rich and the poor.

What's worse is the fact that the majority of our citizenry has bought into this scenario and doesn't see their real intangible assets and worth as the major equity we as a nation possess. Setting up our standards and visions with this defined limitation has crippled us and allowed those who have been corrupted by the power and influence of monetary wealth to become the gatekeepers of our dreams and aspirations.

We don't have to fear the suffering of being tangibly poor because we've already given up our freedom to become intangibly wealthy; to contribute and be enriched to a healthy growing society. The class struggle between the rich and the poor is predetermined by the limited definition we reduce being rich and poor to be. The freedoms and principles our nation was founded on didn't proclaim that the way to life, liberty, and the pursuit of happiness would be through a checkbook. The fact is, the pillars we were founded on convey the exact opposite concept. Our currency is noted with the inscription "In God We Trust," not "whoever has the biggest trust fund gets to make the rules." The get-rich-and-rule mentality has been the undoing of our nation for decades now. It is the precept to becoming a tyrannical nation that zaps all the will and hope from our tired, hungry, and poor and leads the majority into apathy about directing their future and growing their dreams and aspirations. It fortifies a nation that feeds fodder from the top down, where mediocrity is the best we can hope for. This instant self-gratification creates the two class mentality of haves and have nots that steers our entire society down the same cattle shoot. Instead of opening up our minds to enhancing and investing in the world we live in for the greater good of the human race, we continually look for instant return on our own input without regard to growing by giving and not expecting in return.

True value and wealth evolve out of dedicating our time and energy to creating a community that gives all its citizenry the tools to visualize, aspire to, and generate a land that serves and replenishes abundance and opportunity perpetually—without concern for self-gratification. The magnetism and attraction to growing the reality of our dreams comes from investing and giving from the talents we're gifted with and/or ascertained along the highway of life.

The truly wealthy who get this experiment we call America realize that in order to perpetuate the precedent of abundance we have accumulated for the past 230-plus years, we have to give back and cultivate an open, free-thinking culture that wields its strength by staying united yet encompassing diversity, ingenuity, vision, trust, and faith to utilize the resources we've been afforded. To steward over this vast land of manifest destiny with the ideal that all our people have the freedom to become contributing factors to this land of plenty. To conquer the dichotomy we have instituted over the last half century by once again becoming a nation of producers and innovators. To care, nurture, and serve people that put the wealth of our community ahead of our own personal wealth. To continue down the path of hoarding and consuming is to expedite a destiny with oblivion and extinction.

Take a look around you at all of Mother Nature, God's creation, and you'll witness that to grow and thrive in an environment all the principles of that environment need to work in concert with one another. Every aspect of a healthy environment recognizes and respects the beauty each individual contributor brings to the whole, and at the same time allows for the growth of all positive attributes. There are a multitude of classes—there is individual glory and humility—there is mutual respect and admiration for individual contribution that nurtures and grows the total environment. Concurrently, there is a weeding-out process of the characteristics that become lethal and detrimental to the existence of that environment. One contributor never has reign over all, and when headed on that path the whole circumvents to prevent its demise and preserve the ability to foster new growth. We are part of our own environment, and we must be responsible to it in order to survive, prosper, and leave a continuing legacy that states, "During our watch we served to enrich those who will follow; we make history by our actions and the true richness we part this mortality with will lie in the realization that we forwarded what was entrusted to us with a clearer roadmap for those who will follow; that the future will hold more hope, faith, understanding, humility, trust, opportunity, and love than when we acquired it; that all the inhabitants of our land will be afforded those pillar principles set by those who went before us and expanded on during our tenure."

The rich and the poor recognize and nurture the best attributes encumbered by both to form a new definition of the United States, opening up vision, unity, and the will of the one who created the land we set foot on. Classes put limitations on the American Dream, and the timeless unique beauty of our history has, is, and always will reside in our ability to rise beyond those limitations to benefit all our people and open up the bounty we hold to the rest of humanity.

By serving and giving each other the opportunity to succeed, we live the message as an example to the rest of the world of what freedom truly means. We don't coerce our ideals on our neighbors; we open up avenues to afford our neighbors a better way of living in the spirit in which we are afforded the same opportunities. We hold the potential to true wealth; it begins to evolve, distinguishing the way we define being rich. Do we "trust in God" or do we build the biggest trust fund?

Single Room School House Springfield VT

EDUCATION, A PRIVILEGE OR A RIGHT?

ᏬᎧ

I have listed some of the components that comprise elementary and secondary education in recent years as well as some of the issues they have roused on our society:

- Public/charter/private
- No Child Left Behind Act— mandates verses funding
- Administration: business at the expense of our children's future
- Federal and state working in tandem
- PTO/PTA and other organizations that involve students, parents, and teachers
- Reading, writing, arithmetic—the 3 Rs of fundamental learning
- Pricing our children's future right out of the ballpark
- How far we have put our youth behind the eight ball for the gratification and comfort of now
- Mis-education: teaching our kids inadequate fundamental thought processes that will hinder them tackling tomorrow's challenges, pushing them all down the same cattle shoot to "market" a success story that has no substance behind it
- training and continuing education we are affording our teachers, holding them accountable through merit and incentives based on expanding their careers

Can't we make the teaching profession a noble aspiration once more and justly reward quality that propels our future to a higher standard. Aren't the true heroes and role models of our society those who lay out the foundation for our future by training the potential that will form this reality?

How can we mortgage away our community by pricing post-secondary education at a level that either leaves tomorrow's leaders in huge debt or is only affordable to those who come from affluent backgrounds? I contend that education in the United States should be both a right and a privilege. Our youth should inherit the opportunity to better both themselves and society. Upon learning the core disciplines for functioning and contributing, they'll open up opportunity to apply themselves so they can continue to pursue their passions, dreams, and aspirations; in turn, society will benefit from their enlightenment. They will be in a position to give back what they've been gifted (using community service as collateral in lei of putting these individuals into a financial hole as soon as they graduate). By using incentives that benefit the entire community, we will convey the premise that higher education is a privilege of those who seek the responsibility of bettering our future.

Just as freedom carries the price tag of responsibility, the same familiar independence that a quality education affords comes with the responsibility of giving back what we've received. This is the essence of higher education and the core of how we continue to be educated throughout our lives. We learn that the more we are taught, the more there is to teach and learn; education becomes open-ended and continuous. What's more evident is the need to foster this philosophy by using incentive and insight rather than manipulation, debt, and profit at the expense of a brighter tomorrow.

As we advance in our continuing education we learn that education is the key lifelong investment that opens doors to prosperity and eternal wealth. Yet it boils back down to two cardinal principles that connect all of us in this American Dream: that relationships with our neighbors and understanding rather than being understood leads us to a higher everlasting existence that mutually benefits our society and ourselves at the same time.

Education is a lifetime proposition; it is the formula that unlocks all our potential and allows us to pursue our dreams and visions. While it has been believed that every citizen has the right to an education, from the benefactor's standpoint it is definitely a privilege to be educated in order to enhance humankind. In other words every citizen of this country deserves the opportunity to foster a basic education in order to become a productive part of society. What becomes clearer as we progress through grade school is the fact that educating ourselves to advance our contributing factor in the world is definitely a privilege to be taken seriously and when taken advantage of opens up unlimited opportunity to those who seek and respect the value it offers throughout a lifetime (priceless).

Our prize asset as a nation is our people and the knowledge base they acquire and impart over a lifetime. So why is it we cost most of our potential success right out of the market when it comes to providing a quality education? Shouldn't we be investing most heavily in this area, from funding the mandates established with a No Child Left Behind mentality to making higher education affordable to those who seek to make a greater contribution? I'm definitely not advocating a free ride through the system, but haven't we missed the bigger picture when structuring our education process?

It starts with our initial formal training in elementary school; we make our own foundation by utilizing the right to be educated and view education as a privilege and blessing towards creating a more prosperous tomorrow. The way in which we show our gratitude to learning is to open our minds and positively absorb each lesson taught, expanding our knowledge base, then utilizing lessons learned to benefit the environment around us. We give back as we advance, and we keep driving towards broadening our experiences. Put in a different context, the more we learn, the more we learn there is to learn.[iv]

In order to build from our education we must use it and convey it in our daily living. If we hoard what we learn and fail to impart its benefits through our action—use the skill set we acquire—we cut ourselves off from the true benefits of being educated and our quality of life becomes diminished. The cliché "the mind is a terrible thing to waste"[v] holds so much truth; the average person can see through the maturity displayed whether or not he or she views education as a right or a privilege. You see, if you keep an open mind and continually promote education on all levels, you start to understand that the "right" part of education lies in the opportunity to learn, and the "privilege" part of education commences when we seize that opportunity; run with our passions, gifts, and abilities; and fine tune our skill set as well as develop new skills to make the environment we live in more productive and beneficial. In other words, as we advance in our learning we end up teaching and opening up avenues for others to realize new concepts. This becomes a hallmark of our character and the seedlings to our legacy as a society. If we are open to being educated and educating throughout our lives, we will be an invaluable commodity for those who lack this opportunity; they will be enticed to seek and embark on this right.

Again, education holds the keys to enlightenment and elevating humanity to a higher place. To value education as the vehicle that will allow you to acquire your American Dream is to understand the privilege that education has to offer once we unlock the door of opportunity and step across the threshold of learning into the room of challenge and adventure. Yes, education is an investment, and it takes sacrifice, commitment, focus, resources, and dedication to become educated in the field each of us ventures into. It opens up a world of possibilities that can only be explored if we continue to nurture our minds, hearts, and souls to learn what still needs to unfold and be disseminated to benefit society with this newfound knowledge.

Once more, why do we price our greatest potential asset right out of the market? Why do we hold so much of our citizenship under ransom and create so much more corruption, hostility, and waste? Why do we choose to manipulate the masses and fail to invest in educating our future society so they have resources to tackle meaningful long-term issues that will enhance and grow our society? By giving all our siblings the chance and privilege to learn and contribute to a more glorious future, we would be investing in our future as a nation rather than mortgaging our future away.

It begins with restructuring are elementary and secondary education curriculums to bring quality education to every neighborhood and community in America. This can only be accomplished by dedicating enough resources to attract and retain qualified, professional faculty and arming them with the tools needed to harness the raw potential that lies within our leaders of tomorrow. From a city, state, and national viewpoint, why can't we make teaching the noble profession it deserves to be—that most civil countries have be doing for centuries. Our society as a whole suffers from a sickness and addiction that allows professional athletes/entertainers to be paid eons more than what we compensate those who devote their careers to molding the real future of our society. How do we stand a chance of tending to our current challenges when we pay hundreds of millions of dollars to young professional athletes and can't even pass basic referendums to upgrade the quality of our education systems in our communities? We have lost touch with the reality we have evolved from, and at the pace we are going it will be a hard sell to get us back on the right track.

We are currently digging our way to oblivion with the mindset that it's acceptable to endorse a three hundred dollar–night at the ballpark, yet we can't afford to outfit our schools with basic reading, writing, and arithmetic supplies. How is it that the NCAA can generate millions upon millions of dollars on the backs of some of our most talented and potentially inspiring youth, yet the cost of being a college student leaves a graduate up to one hundred thousand dollars in debt coming out of undergraduate school? Don't we have the education equation perversely inverted?

Why does the government only invest a maximum of $6,900 into a Pell grant for eligible students per year to aid in college tuition, and then stand idly by when the cost of tuition on average at a state school has risen to $25,000 per year (private schools upwards of $50,000)? These higher institutions of learning are our chief research and development as well as think-tank laboratories that outfit our future knowledge in tackling the challenges of today and tomorrow. Wouldn't it be more prudent and wise to invest heavily in preparing those who will eventually be responsible for cleaning up and turning around our mess in order to provide not only for themselves but to ensure the dreams of their offspring have the chance to become reality? Isn't the essence of education, as mentioned earlier, affording the next generation the ability to think for themselves so they can live and prosper with abundance; in turn, doesn't the community become enriched by their contributions?

History educates us to the fact that if we lose sight of this concept and manipulate education as a tool for the controlling affluent, sooner or later a once thriving, growing society will sicken and perish leaving way for a new community willing to educate and be educated to the benefit of improving the lifestyle of that whole community, society, race of people. The empires of yesterday have gone by the wayside because they grew old in their thinking and stuck in their ways. America has been successful because at every turn in our country's history we have reeducated ourselves and converted lessons learned into knowledge gained for our entire society as well as for those seeking a positive, brighter path in the world. Education whether formal or informal is the key that unlocks opportunity and offers the challenge to form reality out of dreams and vision; it is the catalyst and engine that propels us to that reality and affirms our faith in achieving what was once thought to be impossible. Education is the intangible wealth we acquire that drives us on to eternity; it is a privilege developed from a right that with age becomes wisdom for those who seek its candor. With it we are limitless, we continue and persist; without it we are limited, we merely survive and over time perish

Deepwater Horizon BP Gulf of Mexico Oil Rig
Explosion

THE DISREGARD FOR OUR ENVIRONMENT

☙❧

Over the past half century we have had basically no concern for our environment when it comes to creating convenience and comfort for ourselves. We spare no expense to please our wants, and at the same time we are irresponsible for the affects our efforts have on the environment.

Pollution of all types has become as big an issue as the actual products we manufacture and consume. The template we have laid out for developing industrial nations to build upon doesn't bode well for our planet. Over the last few decades and especially since the dawn of the new millennium, we have become increasingly conscious of the adverse effects our lifestyle has rendered on the environment. The "Go Green" initiatives have gained much momentum in the private sector, and government on all levels has become involved and associated with these efforts as well. Integration between these two sectors involving incentives and backed by grassroots support will go a long way toward mending our past practices and opening up a new way of living that cultivates a moral sense of responsibility and commitment to each other in our society as well as the world at large.

By making conscious efforts to improve the quality of our environment and to restore a vibrant, growing ecosystem, we open ourselves up to acquire new knowledge and technology for benefiting our individual lifestyles; in turn; we gain a cleaner flourishing community and nation. We will be taking major steps towards fostering a more wholesome venue for tomorrow's generation. In addition, we will be engaging with the rest of the world to create similar efforts, advocating the practice that everyone has the responsibility to contribute and act in a fashion that promotes health and prosperity as well as opportunity for all humanity.

We are part of the same human race; regardless of our differences in ideology, philosophy, faith, and citizenship; and the environment does not delineate with regard to country and power structures. What I'm trying to convey is this one cardinal fact with relation to the environment—we all have a responsibility to live with the utmost stewardship and integrity when it comes to protecting and enhancing our environment. Each of us is either part of the problem or part of the solution; there is no gray area regarding this issue. We as a "nation under God" have been gifted this earth and all the bounty it entails; we must think through reasonably the prudent actions we take on an everyday basis—as to how we are affecting the planet we live on. Are we living selfishly, just concerned with making our sphere of living comfortable for us in the here and now? Are we promoting convenience for profit at the expense of our existence down the road? What is the reasoning for the actions we take? Do we consider the effects we are having on the society at large when we venture into our goals and dreams, or are we shortsighted and only thinking about personal gain and prosperity? To truly gain for ourselves we must consciously plan and partake in life with the benefit of the majority at the heart of our endeavors.

We are not going to have the answers to a better environment all at once, and we cannot paralyze our efforts to establish a better life for our nation by forgoing initiatives until we have all the answers with relation to how we can best serve the people and our environment at the same time. No, what I am advocating with regard to our environment is that we act morally with a bit of forethought as to how we can protect and strengthen our environment as we go about our daily living.

It all starts with how we live each day and how we act towards this land that we have been blessed to inhabit. If we can take the time to factor in the environment with how we conduct our business, think how much more aware we will be of working with and for the rest of the community. Then multiply that by all the communities in our society, and we start to see how each drop of water in the pail plays an essential role in the makeup of the total body of water. How we consume, what we do with the resources we have, and why we are driven to accomplish what we do determines our impact on the environment in every possible dimension. If our motivation is primarily driven by the bottom line with convenience, comfort, and self-indulgence as the main goals of our production, then we are only shortchanging our long-term growth—acquiring temporary gain in the tenure of today.

We must be wise enough and flexible enough to learn from how we have grown. Instead of growing old utilizing the same course of action over and over again, we would be better served by serving the community more flexibly—taking into account how we can use what has been harvested and garnered to sustain long-term growth—recreating what we use, consume, and generate in order to keep growing up. If we don't take into consideration the resources we've been afforded when attempting to contribute to the bigger picture, we run the risk of snuffing out the light that allows us to become successful in the first place. In simpler terms, if we disregard the environment we are blessed to be a part of, the environment will surely have the last word with us.

Our intentions may be worthy in pursuing our dreams and aspirations, but we may be blinded to the adverse affects this pursuit will have on the environment. What we need to be consciously aware of is that if we find out we have created challenge in making our goals a reality; we also must bring with us openness, commitment, and faith to confront these challenges so that when reality gets recorded as history we will have worked and served towards maintaining a better opportunity for the future. We have handed on a better environment to tomorrow's stewards.

The environment is directly connected to our health on an individual, community, national, and international level. Like our health, moving forward without regard to maintaining the environment can only compromise how we wish to live and compound the quality of life we leave for those to come after us. We have but one planet, and how we treat it environmentally affects not only our lifestyle as a nation but how we as a nation respect the lifestyle of the rest of the world.

This single issue relates us globally like no other discussed in this book. It transcends boundaries and makes us keenly aware of how interconnected we are in today's world. With progress comes challenge; and in order to grow and promote our democracy and lifestyle, we must first contend with how our lifestyle affects the environment that is shared with the whole world. How we meet our own concerns and needs has a direct correlation to how we are perceived and more importantly how we influence our neighbors both at home and abroad. If we continue to act in a self-serving manner disregarding tomorrow, we will become self-defeating and the rest of humanity will suffer for it. If we start to turn the tide and act with an open willingness and graciousness accounting environmentally for our actions—producing and consuming with the benefit of the majority at the forefront—we might begin to see the strength in living humbly and working toward a better place for all.

The environment and how we adapt to it has a direct association and is a reflection of how we tend to the gifts and opportunities we have been presented from our past. We need to take heed of how those who coveted this land before our time made the best use of what the land has to offer and were responsible enough to steward it so that generations of their civilization would be able to grow and return the bounty, giving the future the chance to sow and reap for the benefit of all. Our outlook towards the environment of today and tomorrow must be perceived and administered to in a realistic similar fashion. Some of the challenge we have created has taken years to manifest, but the way in which we address it needs to be genuine, sincere with commitment that will leave our nation in a better state as time marches on. This is not a quick-fix ordeal; in some instances it will take years to restore a stable, healthy habitat in which to move forward.

As far as global warming is concerned, we have definitely impacted its momentum and we need to initiate plans and actions that work in tandem with the natural fabric of a changing environment. Some of the damage we have caused is irreconcilable, and the natural forces of Mother Nature will have to tend to healing those wounds; but congruently as life moves on we should adjust our lifestyles so that in concert with Mother Nature we contribute to the gentrification rather than the demise of our planet. Surprising as it seems, by changing our attitude and culture in the way we tend to our living, we will open up whole new industries of opportunity. We will create a new morality that will nurture and grow a prosperous, healthy community. Our nation will thrive once more with optimistic vision that redirects the difficulties of today into the opportunities of tomorrow.

The environment and how we regard it is integrated into the fabric of our Constitution and affects every aspect of our freedom from health to energy to the economy to our morality as a nation. If, nationally, we believe in the plight of our cause, we can clearly see that good stewardship to the environment transforms to moral, civil, and biological responsibility to all our citizenship. In turn, contributing to a healthy environment serves the needs and desires of people to live in harmony with the rest of God's creations. We reflect our Creator's love for us by exemplifying that love to one another. We did not create our initial environment; it was gifted to us with the purpose of sustaining life. But we have been given the freedom to choose how we grow and give back to the One who has endowed us with the very gift of life. We can use our talents to multiply, flourish, and take delight in the bounty bestowed us—reaching out to one another to afford the same generous environment we have been blessed to partake in. Or we can selfishly squander the opportunities of living and benefiting in a wholesome environment for the sake of limited short-term wealth and control.

In time the latter approach will disconnect us from all the good we have to offer. The environment is like love; we must set it free so that it comes back to us. If we shortchange the habitat we now live in for the temporary comfort and convenience of today and at the expense of a better tomorrow, we will have missed the message of why we were put here in the first place. We, each and every one of us, have the opportunity to contribute and establish a better environment for all of us to live in. Once we start acting nationally with a positive attitude towards our environment, we will unravel the difficulty our past transgressions on the environment have caused and open up new avenues to a healthier planet, renewing the concepts from which we as a nation have evolved.

To disregard the environment is to throw democracy and its moral connotations into the hands of evil, to those who are only conscious of their own well-being. What right do we have to disregard a gift so precious that without it we as a people would cease to exist? Can we really afford to be a major contributor to the demise of the human race because of our inequities to an atmosphere that has graciously enabled us to act in such a way? Don't we owe it to each other to invest in a world that provides unlimited possibility due to the fact that in our actions we respect and preserve the very atmosphere that affords us the luxury to pursue our passions? Should we not act with humility when treading on ground that's been blessed for us from the beginning? On our watch we should learn from the past and utilize our resources of the present to outfit a healthier environment for tomorrow filled with promise, beauty, and unending love for the inhabitants that will light the way of the future.

MEDICAL ADVANCE AND ITS LIMITED ALLOCATION

∽

It seems that greed and profit are expeditiously infiltrating the decay of every aspect of our society including the implementation of the medical advances that will enhance the proliferation of both the quality and longevity of life. By chasing a greenback for so long and allowing economics to drive the health and medical profession as a business first rather than having the mandate be "invest in medicine for the preservation of quality living supplemented by adequate economic resources," we have stunted the potential to make major medical breakthroughs available to our society on an equitable basis.

Time and time again we hear of doctors leaving the profession, research programs going belly up because insurance is too high and funding has dried up. The underlying factor of overall greed and the resulting lack of trust has driven us to this result. We are all guilty of contributing to this end because on many varying levels we have lost focus on the purpose of why we have a medical and health profession. We cut off our nose to spite our face because we lose sight of the end goal of medicine and its advances—mainly, to promote health and enhance quality of living.

When we have the knowledge, talent, and ability to make inroads against such diseases as cardiovascular disease, cancer, AIDS, and various other life-threatening, debilitating illnesses, why should the barrier of economics artificially derail the resolution and implementation of administering the cures for these diseases? On some deep level these life altering illnesses exist as a test to how we tend to our neighbors. Do we value their lives as much as our own, or do we cave into the economics of our times and rationalize our lack of caring as an economic casualty? With so many resources being poured into the technological advances of diagnosing illness and trying to implement the adage "an ounce of prevention is worth a pound of cure," we seem to drop the ball when it comes to allocating these resources and educating the majority of our society.

This is primarily due to the facts of letting money and insurability stand in the way of true medical (and ironically economic) progress. By interpreting the funding needed to allocate medical advances as an expense rather than an investment that will warrant a healthier, more prosperous society in the long run, we are casting our society away to a wealthy few who are the only ones affluent enough to endure and remain healthy (though in most cases morally bankrupt). What good is it as a nation to segregate who is entitled to receive care due to the financial balance sheet they hold when most of the illness begotten is due to arbitrary circumstances? Further, what good is it to promote democracy in other areas of our lives if we treat medicine as a privilege of the rich, denying the rest of our society the chance to pursue a healthy lifestyle because they can't afford to pay for it? Doesn't our Declaration of Independence decree that all people are created equal and should be endowed with certain unalienable rights, which include the right to liberty, justice, and the pursuit of happiness?[vi] Furthermore, doesn't this infer that to pursue these freedoms we should have the right of health to begin with?

Going further back in history, didn't the Good Samaritan set the bar as to how we should treat our neighbor when he tended to the beaten Jew on the side of the road?[vii] Did he not invest in his fellow man out of necessity and not out of greed or condition? And did he not act out of love, which expects nothing in return because it was love that afforded him his own health and the ability to act in the manner that he did? Why in this day and age do we think we are owed a return on everything we endeavor; aren't we wealthier and healthier when our acts of charity brighten the whole of society at large? The only return we should be hoping for is that those receiving the enrichment of advanced medical care will be enlightened enough to pass along similar opportunity to others who are in need when they can position themselves to do so. The unity in the medical profession must reside in viewing the benefit of advancing the health of our nation and the world with the gifts and abilities obtained as a responsibility and an obligation to assist our neighbor in times of need. The return we receive will come in fostering a healthier, more independent nation that remains thankful for the blessing of health by gifting back and contributing to those who are less fortunate.

Financing these advances is an investment we make in ourselves as a community, and the trust that it represents can only grow if it is shared and not hoarded. We need to be willing to sacrifice everything if we have faith and trust that by doing so we as a people will nurture a better wealth in the long run. To gain medically at the expense of the majority is to boast a morality that holds no value; but to invest in advancing medicine to create a better lifestyle for the community is to transcend mortality and reach out to another's soul. What good does it do us to conquer the challenges faced in medicine today if we can only impart these advances to a select few? Judging from our history and the wisdom that was used to defeat smallpox, tuberculoses, diphtheria, and other plagues that threatened us in the past, the true benefit of discovering the cure to these diseases was realized in the access with which these cures were delivered to the public. We don't have to contend with these diseases today because our ancestors focused on finding and administering a cure to the masses without regard for consideration. Their reward has come from the realization that these diseases are but history today. The prevailing attitude and dedication of former generations need be applied today when confronting the plagues that are prevalent today. We must cherish life and health to the point that when medicine develops a cure or breakthrough to major sickness or illness, we waste no time in administering it without discrimination. The wealth we gain by approaching all life's health as an investment can't be ignored because the intrinsic wealth gained by stamping out the illnesses of today is the biggest return humankind could ever expect or hope for.

AIG Building in New York NY

PROPPING UP THE ECONOMY ON BIG BUSINESS WHILE MAIN STREET FALLS APART

∽

We as a country have yet to address the underlying cause of our current economic woes. The immorality in the form of greed, profit at the expense of our neighbor, immediate gratification, and the unwillingness to invest in our future by sacrificing some comfort today has lead us to our knees in a rapid succession of historical events. And blindly trying to cover ourselves with Band-aids to cure our self-inflicted wounds without taking the time and energy to identify and tend to the root causes will lead us farther down the road to destruction, at an accelerated pace.

It is time to face the mirror as a nation (rich, poor, healthy, sick, employed, unemployed, consumer, producer, spender, savor, homeowner, renter, CEO, destitute) as citizens of this "one nation under God"[viii] and search deep into our souls to see where each and every one of us can make amends for our shortcomings and identify where we are truly at. Are we still willing to sacrifice and compromise for the greater good of the nation (our brothers and sisters)? Are we willing to commit to well thought out, long-term vision that will lead to health, prosperity, wealth, and unity for our society? Are we willing to create value and discipline in the way we go about achieving our new vision? And are we open and willing enough to trust, invest in, and work with one another to lead us away from the temptations of self-indulgence, self-profit, and excessive comfort so that a greater majority can be afforded the opportunity to grow and develop their gifts and talents benefitting all?

You see, a United States in which we can identify with each other's pain, sacrifice, hard work, needs, and vision for a better tomorrow. Sacrificing and investing in reconciling today's challenges is the only true hope and salvation we have as a nation. Every one of us needs to access where we stand in the present and contribute to the best of our abilities, creating a better base for our successors to develop from and expand on. We need to prune the dead branches and nurture the industrious positive growth of the tree. We need to reinforce and enrich the soil that we are rooted in, and we need to take the log out of our own eye so we can work together toward a clearer vision for the entire community.

We need to prioritize what is a need and what is a want; when we can provide a comfort for the majority as far as needs are concerned (food, clothing, shelter, health, and education), we will be on the road to healing as a nation. Don't misconstrue unity with uniformity—the goal is not to have everyone be fat, dumb, and happy, for ignorance and bliss can accomplish this throughout the economic spectrum. No, the goal is to afford as much of our citizenry as possible the opportunity to use and enhance their gifts, abilities, and talents in an avenue that far exceeds self-satisfaction; that parleys and benefits a higher quality of life for as many in the community and society as possible.

Each of us has exponentially more to offer than what we currently commit to. It is up to each of us to awaken our consciences, get outside ourselves, and approach life in the present with others in the forefront benefiting from the merits in which we serve. At first some will need to be provided for in a variety of ways and those who can accommodate these needs have to step up with resources (without precondition of gaining from an adverse situation) and nurture our neighbors back to health. By taking on this responsibility we will encourage health, wealth, prosperity, and freedom. The more inundated we become in this environment, the more contagious and promoting its benefits become, not only to those in need but to those who are needed.

True community starts with a belief and passion that the population at large is only as strong as its weakest members. This democratic society only thrives and grows when the majority of hearts are centered on manifesting a bounty to be shared by all its members. The collective positive force that runs common through a society's lifeblood is founded on values of trust, honesty, respectability, accountability, integrity, and citizenship. It becomes enriched through the diversity of talents and gifts each of us contributes to the cause, and we all become enhanced by the dedication, openness, and character we educate ourselves with in the yearning to foster a better country.

We are gifted our present-day stewardship on the backs of those who endowed themselves to make our nation a better place so we who wish to can create even better tomorrows. We acknowledge first and foremost that our lives are gifted to us from the start. We are given the freedom to choose which path we wish to explore and which passions we plan to devote our lives to. We as a nation ought to be thankful for the opportunity and challenge we been blessed with. To show our gratitude, we must assess our own inventory on a daily basis and commit to developing to our fullest those talents and abilities that tap our potential, creating kinetic results and instilling the faith, confidence, and character that continually drive us to greater success for the society with which we help create.

If each of us stopped for a few minutes each day to listen to our consciences and act with our hearts towards mentoring a better day in the environment that surrounds us—if we were to get up and start living today as if it were our last day on earth—we would awaken living for the day and amazingly accomplish much more than we bargain for when we attack each day with mediocrity and complacency. If we are willing to go through the rough times with positive motivation, think how blessed we'll be when the sea of tribulation subsides and we continue to focus on a purpose to enlighten tomorrow for a greater part of humanity.

We live in an age that lends itself to unthinkable wealth and prosperity for all humankind because of the pilgrimage that's been taken by those who believed in America's spirit—not boastful, but humble in victory; not distraught, but gracious in defeat—understanding and conscientious of what makes us all members of the same race. Even in the current domestic struggles, we should take the time to evaluate where our true convictions lie, for it is in our darkest hours that our true character surfaces; and it is through honest reflection of how we act during these depressed times that we can measure our growth and maturity. If we let history repeat itself over and over again, we reveal just the mortal human aspect of our being; but if we can find it in our hearts to surrender control of our destiny to a greater cause and obey the principles and commandments that will lead us to this cause, we just might find wisdom through our experience enough to light the way to a more enduring day. We might expose the genuine spirit that has resonated throughout this land since the time of its first inhabitants.

You see, our country predates its independence symbolized by the ring and crack of the Liberty Bell—the bell personifies our spirit of unity and independence as well as our diversity and imperfections that continually leverage and challenge us to become better than we were yesterday. Our forefathers had mountains to climb that were as high as the ones we face today when reviewed in the context of their day. We were founded from victory over the mightiest empire on earth, and the next day had to find ways of commerce in the new world. We were indebted to the allies who now had a vested interest in us. In addition we had the internal chaos that comes with developing sovereignty as well as reconciling with those who were here before us who once roamed this land and still inhabited the greater part of the frontier.

You see, living in the present and dealing with the here and now was as challenging then as it is now. It was those who had the fortitude, vision, faith, courage, wisdom, and serenity to act for the greater good of our new civilization that inaugurated the pillars of where we stand today. And all the great leaders and servants who collectively have formed the citizenship of this great land since that heralded beginning have kept the torch of freedom and democracy burning brightly through good weather and bad. They lived and live with moral fiber that breathes with the fabric of our country: a purpose-driven society that generates fellowship by growing stronger through community rather than through individual self-righteous effort. A nation that's beholden to the truths that have paved the way for such bounty and abundance, yet never forgets the route taken to get there and is always willing to offer a helping hand to those in need.

We are a united people of immense variety and diversity that even through these unprecedented economic times should give thanks and take stock from where we've come, from knowing that if we persevere with forethought, ingenuity, vision, and awareness that we are all Americans and each of us contributes to our success, we will grow and venture to new heights in the days ahead. We will pursue the legacy we've been endowed and entrusted with and we will bequeath to our inheritors a land that's been stewarded with the utmost care and leaves plenty of untapped bounty for generations to come. We can only make an impact on our generation in the here and now; it is up to us to steward with reverence, lead by example, and serve for the greater good of those who will light the path when we leave. If this means enduring some grapes of wrath then we should be so fortunate to be asked to take on that challenge. Those with a true propensity to live the American Dream will commit to working with fortitude to a goal that envisions unlimited abundance at the top—a return to the philosophy that I can achieve my dream and so can my neighbor; we will both be better for accomplishing our feats.

With renewed leadership that is willing to harness the strengths of all Americans and assist in providing the potential to succeed, we should all come to the table with contributing hearts, open minds, and the willingness to make the effort in generating moral values that reinforce the cornerstone of where we have come as well as expand the horizon of where we are going as a nation. Let us restore the "Trust in God" part of our currency so that we deal going forward in good faith among ourselves. In turn, this goodwill restores the faith and respect the world has in us as a true leader and ambassador to humanity. Our freedom will once again ring from within, and the sound waves will act as a catalyst for the rest of the free world to chime in. If we reconcile our relationships first, we can generate enough resources to resolve the most challenging scenarios. This is the essence of the United States of America, and on this platform we embark, progressing to a more sovereign and solvent vision of a brighter tomorrow.

Border Patrol Wall in Southwest USA

ILLEGAL IMMIGRATION AND THE SWEATSHOP MENTALITY THAT BOTH BANKRUPTS AND FUELS ITS ILLEGALITY

Throughout the eighties and nineties as well as through the present decade, illegal immigration has put a huge strain on the underpinnings of the economy. This has been especially evidenced along our border states where we have spent many resources in combating this issue with only marginal success. Compound this with the additional resources drained in providing services for these aliens and then multiply it by the lost tax revenue base for the jobs being worked under the table. This is only the economic damage that's sustained. Analyze this crisis further and you see that the major players in this dilemma are the employers who keep illegal workers between a rock and a hard place for the sake of their own profit. It has been estimated that nearly eleven million illegal immigrants inhabit our country[ix] and provide much of the low-tech service employment which some say could not be replaced by legal citizens in this nation.

To me this reeks of the highest degree of manipulation of our own society by a small percentage of the whole. I often wonder and question those who have immigrated legally into this country and have more empathy to the current situation. On one hand they can relate to the want of a better lifestyle that these aliens long for; but on the other hand they see how manipulated they are and in some cases how depleting it can be to their everyday environment.

Our freedom, which is what entices those wanting to pursue their dreams in this land, must convey that this opportunity to succeed entails responsibility from and to all parties concerned. We must approach immigration with the same set of principles that have allowed our current citizenry the Constitutional rights to foster such a free lifestyle.

For a nation that touts human rights all over the world and has even gone to war over similar treatment of humanity in other parts of the world, a nation that has passed legislation deterring such sweatshop mentality and has had a long-standing feud with the most populous country in the world with regard to their treatment of their own citizenship (China), we sure turn a blind eye to the same shortcomings in our own backyard. We have really dropped the ball on this one for several decades, and as the problem has become ever more entwined with the decay of our total morality, we have the gall to sink millions of dollars into building a wall that pathetically is suppose to keep the "illegal immigrants" out. The real trash in this situation already exists in this country and sad to say is a part of our citizenry. Those who harbor for their own gain at the expense of these illegal immigrants as well as their neighbors are the real source of the problem. Instead of propping up a wall at the taxpayers' expense, why don't we tear down the wall of ignorance and thoughtfully invest in correcting the disconnect we have let fester in our land? Further, why don't we coalition with our neighboring countries to raise the wealth and knowledge of living so that immigration becomes a natural flow and is not just predicated on material gain and manipulation and greed?

For too long we have conveyed a double standard with ourselves and the rest of the world; we expound upon being the most civil country on earth, yet we fuel our growth engine by manipulating illegal immigrants to work the menial jobs that provide us this so-called civil state. Our homes, the food that is harvested, the landscaped environment we reside in, the hotels we stay at, the gas we get pumped into our vehicles, the fast food that we purchase—all has been built primarily over these past decades on the backs of illegal immigration. While we tout equality and fight for human rights all over the globe, we struggle at home to make the effort to live under the same values we preach to others. This double standard erodes the integrity and leverage we have when negotiating with fellow citizens and neighbors around the world. It also creates animosity among those we've taken advantage of and those who try to live by what they believe and preach.

To stem this tide of negativity we must start to make everyone accountable for his or her own freedom to pursue life, liberty, and happiness. This entails being responsible to the society that affords us the opportunity to embark on this pursuit. We need to reconcile our present relationships with those who are present and alien in this country today based on the fairest criteria established up by focus groups that contain a cross section of our citizenship (somewhat along the lines of how our jury duty selection process presently works). This would allow input for creating new policy on this aspect of the immigration process to come from those most empathic and affected, citizens of our society.

Next, we have to address with a stern hand those who seek to gain profit from the continual use of illegal labor. If a crackdown in this regard creates challenge to the lifestyle we have become accustomed to, then it will also provide opportunity for growth and rejuvenation to those legitimately seeking to find a better way. The only way to honor those who immigrated to this country legally in the past and have made this country their home is to hold the standards to which we live and grow with to same integrity that allowed them to work towards their dreams. Too many times for far too long we have rationalized away what's been fostered in this country because our comfort level might be affected if we forge change that would legitimize and constitute a clearer path towards citizenship. Those who truly believe in this democracy we call the United States of America have the obligation and responsibility to be the best stewards we can to all that we can for as long as we can so that the ensuing generation has a trail to follow and an inspiration to create for tomorrow a more amicable way. An enticing freedom that persuades those wanting to live their dreams in this land to do so under the same set of principles that have allowed our citizens the constitutional right to pursue a free lifestyle.

To be a legal immigrant or citizen of the USA means one is willing to make the sacrifice and garner the responsibility entailed in gaining the right to freely pursue a better lifestyle, as well as to understand the history of where we as a nation have come from and to advocate the ideals that make living here so attractive. This process may not seem fair and equitable at first to those who wish to take on the dream; but in order to keep the ambition alive for others to follow, an orderly process need be applied. This allows the greater good of the whole to invoke the best in every citizen who aspires to contribute to it.

Sadly, there is a lack of respect for this quality of life within the citizenship that has already been established in this country.

More people who have been granted citizenship—through birth—in this land don't truly comprehend, and do take for granted; the privilege afforded them to live in a land that holds so much bounty, opportunity, freedom, and promise. We don't see the charter that was set before us and gave us a guide to pilgrimage toward enlightenment. The bigger lessons in our history show that to gain we must serve, and by serving everyone stands to gain. To contribute by sharing wealth rather than hoarding or squandering it secures and expands the pillars we as a nation have grown from. We extend the same hand that was lent to us from our predecessors when we began our stewardship; so that the American Dream becomes more clairvoyant as time marches into the future.

We are a diverse population and as such are more open to all the advantages and disadvantages that come with this territory. We have the opportunity to fine tune and grow the foundation our forefathers set for us, in turn giving more people the chance to grow and prosper by working, sacrificing, gifting, and visioning a greater heartland for all our neighbors. This country has survived and grown from generations that have witnessed the bounty of our great land and longed for the opportunity to create a better lifestyle for those who inhabit our shores. The hope that America has attracted from around the world throughout the generations, that has fueled the fires of expansion for over two hundred thirty years and has given back to those we have seen as in need, can only perpetuate into the future if it remains founded on the core principles it has evolved from. If we lose the roots from which we've been enriched for the sake of temporary gain, we lose the course for where we are headed and start to wither away. To disconnect from our past will expedite us into the darkness of tomorrow rather than draw others into the light of our day. We will become a fading page in history that over time will be remembered more for our demise than for the salvation we once granted the world. To reverse our fall into the great abyss of history, we need to take stock in our actions of today, reach outside our comfort zone, and prepare our steps to a brighter morrow by committing to the growth of our nation and not just to our individual bottom lines. What good is it to gain the "world" if it is at the world's expense we profit?

AMERICA'S ADDICTION TO DRUGS (ILLEGAL AND LEGAL)

In the 1960s while the Civil Rights movement was creating chaos and violence throughout our nation, another subculture was rearing its counterproductive head in the mainstream of our society in the form of illegal substance abuse, creating an era that forever changed our perception of what is conventional and abiding. The hippie years were full of plenty of sex, drugs, and rock and roll, where revolting against what was once the mainstream ideal became the new ideal of the age. The black market infiltrated not only the urban cities of our land but branched into the sprawling suburbia that was redefining the landscape. We were being deluged by the underground importation and distribution of illegal drugs at a pace and volume that if tracked as a legitimate business would be quite competitive in the Fortune 500.

This challenge to our way of life has been demonizing our spirit since the 1960s. It has worked its way into our music, our attitude, our economy, and our future—having an adverse affect on the vibrancy, production, and innovation of our society. Additionally, it has conveyed the perception to our neighbors that in a morally decaying society without regard for discipline relating to our intangible wealth, we have become a bastion for recreational drug use as well as market for big-time unlawful commerce in drug trafficking.

By the time we deemed it necessary to direct major resources to this challenge, the horse was leaving a burning barn, so to speak. The infestation had already been rooted, much like mercantilism was established when we were developing under British rule. The money we threw at the problem was as much a drain on our society and economy as the issue itself. The superficial approach we took to this systemic problem and its lack of result showed how infiltrated and rooted this subculture had become—ingrained into the fabric of our lives. The supply chain had been entrenched into every part of our society, unlike Prohibition where the government sought remedy by gaining control of the distribution of alcohol (reaping the economic benefits of legalizing a drug). Our government and law enforcement were completely outcast from acquiring any upside in attempting to corral and contract to the business of dealing, importing, manufacturing, and dispensing these illegal substances. Instead of concentrating on educating our public to the adverse affects and counterproductivity getting involved in this illegal industry would ultimately yield, we allowed the dynamic mirage of getting rich quick by dealing, getting away by using, and reaching utopia by accepting this lifestyle and condoning this false culture to be manipulated on our youth. We lost many major battles trying to expunge this infiltrating culture because while expounding on rejecting the legality of the situation in a perverse sort of way, we were giving in on some of the riches and allure this type commerce was capturing in our country. What we failed to convey is that by accepting and indulging in this behavior, we were risking the soul values of our core beliefs.

A whole generation has grown up with drugs having a paramount influence on how we perceive and are perceived in life. Our modern day culture reeks of the challenge we have never seriously stood up to; this has caused way more hardship and disaster to our citizenry than any monetary benefit we could or would have from incorporating this addiction into the mainstream of our society. Yet, in effect, that is what we have done in our present day society.

When you turn on the TV and watch a program, invariably you will be barraged by a multitude of commercials related to curing and resolving a shortcoming with the use of a magic drug or pill. Got a weight problem? Pop a pill and watch the weight vanish before your eyes. Have an ED issue? Take a pill and leave your worries behind. Have an acid reflux problem? Down a pill right before you go off and gorge yourself on any type food your heart desires. The list goes on and on, allowing us to indulge and satisfy our egos, vanity, pleasures, and wants all at the expense of our souls.

We have gotten caught up in the profit of satisfying the wants of the masses because we can exploit their vulnerabilities and cash in on their weaknesses. Having settled for comfort over education and discipline, we don't think twice about the moral implications nor do we concern ourselves with the long-term physical effects of curing what ails us with a drug or warding off reservations with a pill. We don't account for actually living and dealing with the reality presented before us. We become dependent on quick-fix remedies that in the long run complicate our lives and the society we live in.

Instead why don't we approach life with an "all things in moderation" point of view and alter our lifestyle with a little forethought and self-sacrifice? Just look at the pharmaceutical industry today (you can't travel ten miles in my home state of New

Jersey without running into a CVS, Walgreens, or Rite Aide, usually all three at an intersection); we have programmed ourselves into believing that the magic pills are the answer to our problems. The fact of the matter is, we are only compounding most of our problems because we don't take the time to educate ourselves as to the what, why, when, how, and where we've come to experience from our initial problem; and we clearly don't see whom we are affecting in dealing with are problems, expecting immediate gratification from an instant synthetic solution. We are the same generation who grew up ridiculing what adverse effects illegal drugs have had on our society, and yet we have systematically legalized using drugs as an everyday approach to dealing with ordinary living in the same fortuitous manner that drug dealers provide for users who rationalize their escape from everyday reality. We are a physically dependent and sick nation because we have indulged our egos at the expense of our souls. We would rather exist in the comfort of today instead of living with reality and pursuing a purpose of preparing for tomorrow. Legal or illegal, our society has become a prisoner to its own illusion that a pill a day is the eternal way.

For medicine to have a positive long-term effect on our living, we have to first be daring enough to live without it. While seeking cures and remedies to our plaguing difficulties we need to enlighten ourselves to the long-term effects we are striving for when administering and using medicine as part of the cure. Using drugs to resolve disease, ills, or acute shortcomings takes an educated effort by both the user and the provider as to the total environment surrounding each specific situation. In our convenient, addicting society of today, it is too easy to rationalize taking meds as the quintessential remedy to all our pain. As much as it has boosted the drug industry to pie in the sky profit, it has created tenfold the drain on our quality of life. We have become debtors who can't afford the quick fix of false utopia that is constantly marketed to and thrust upon us for the sake of short-term gratification as well as to line other people's pockets. We need to wake up and educate ourselves to the pain of living in reality. Pain is a good thing at times because it lets us know we are alive and kicking, that we can aspire to a new way of thinking in tackling the challenges of today. With a renewed sense of purpose towards making tomorrow brighter for all, we can start to free ourselves from the dependency of addiction and then begin to reconcile with the past and forge a better path to the future: a realistic pilgrimage that sheds light, vision, hope, honesty, and faith on tomorrow; a freedom that allows true Love to conquer where people once manipulated and plundered in addiction. We don't have to keep rewriting history with the same demise of civilization after civilization, but we need to listen with our hearts, think with our minds, and act with our bodies guided by the Spirit that frees all men from their limitation and humbles us to the grace and mercy we seek and long for every day of our mortal lives.[x]

To idolize drugs (legal or illegal) as the answer to our dilemmas is to sell not only ourselves short but to turn our back on our Creator who has given us the freedom to search for cures and remedies through the use of such elements. Medicine, when accompanied with faith and genuine understanding of its intended purpose and when guided by a higher force, can truly be a miraculous gift that enhances a civilization to a higher cause. It can promote a healthy, quality lifestyle that reflects the bounty and beauty of each member's growth and strength in dealing with adversity.

We as a nation need to support one another when it comes to breaking an addiction that roots itself so deeply in our culture. Not only is the withdrawal a physical one, it also lends itself to our spiritual and economical sides. Without a united front to rid this drug-induced decay of our society, we will continue to fight windmills[xi] in vain and lose ground against a plague that perpetually inflicts itself on humanity. A United States that deals in this reality with diversity leverages itself as one body that is capable of curing its drug dependency and then sharing that cure with the world.

OUR LOVE AFFAIR WITH ESCAPING REALITY

As a nation we devote more resources per capita to love affairs that provide brief periods for escaping reality than actually living in the present and turning our dreams into reality. We pursue the chance to drive that ultimate car, marketed as the end all. We endorse a multi-billion dollar movie industry that brings us a few brief hours of escapism and entertainment per movie. Countless dollars are invested in the vacation industry; we earmark money and time to get away to every hot spot around the globe.

The gaming industry has grown dramatically over the past half century, becoming a material part of our gross national product, and that's not including all the illegal gambling that takes place. Millions upon millions of dollars are poured into sporting venues and the events that take place at these facilities. Television has grown from three network channels and a handful of UHF channels in the 1960s to hundreds of channels on cable or dish TV, providing every kind of escapism on earth. In addition to this, the computer and Internet have compounded the availability to seek out programming that allows us to escape from reality for a while. The home improvement industry has become a major national movement, leveraging the masses, assisting in the creation of utopia cribs that contain every convenience under the sun. In addition to all this positive escapism, there are the less glamorous ways people try to escape living such as alcoholism, drug addictions, shopping addictions, those with eating disorders, and those who resort to crime as a basis to fuel their dream world.

The only real way to endure reality is to live it. Let your faith support you through the rough spots, and share the bounty of the fortunes you acquire. Let others take heart in your experiences and bask in theirs as well.[xii] Try to keep an even keel and place volatility in check so when events pin you down to either extremely high emotion or devastatingly low emotion you have a reservoir of experience to help you remain calm, cool, and collected while traversing through your daily living. As good as it gets or as dark as it gets, there is purpose behind every experience we go through, and we can start to realize we are not experiencing life alone. We may not immediately be able to distinguish trees in the forest, but with faith, hope, and time we begin to understand some of the reasoning behind life's occurrences. And when we can't, we must trust in our beliefs, trust in one another that the extreme is but a test and the patience of time will withstand any extremes of the present.

When we deal with the pain of reality and live in the present, we fulfill a new reality—one in which we no longer feel the need to escape or act on impulse to get away or prolong the situation. We begin to mature and relinquish control or the wish for control in order to maintain comfort. Instead, we recognize and utilize what has been granted to us so that reality becomes the vision, and in turn the vision becomes reality. The expression "dream world" usually portrays someone having their cake and eating it, too. We see this as a limited mirage that is perceived as real, yet when we try to become part of it, it vanishes into something completely different. We see and act on perception while all along the truth remains a constant reality. The truth accounts for the whole equation of life—

what we see, what we don't see, what we feel, what we don't feel, in other words the total impact of the whole scenario.

At best, when we take others and their experiences into account and expand our perception of the truth, in time we absorb the truth in our love and action. Truth be told, escapism is much more limited than reality, and the experience of escaping is much less gratifying than living life in the present—the here and now—reality. When you pick up a novel and get lost in your reading, you experience an escape into what seems a more comforting world because you can experience this world from a distance and control the affects it has on you. There comes the time when you finish the story and "poof," you're back to reality. The escape has run its course and cast its emotions through you, allowing you to capture and control the experience as if you were living it yourself. The stark contrast between fiction and reality lies in this one major factor. You see, in reality we don't have control of much, especially when it comes to accounting for the total picture. We have been gifted life, and to think we can both live it and control every aspect of it is to think beyond our means—to escape. Reality is far more adventurous than any place we could ever escape to. The real world is chock full of mountains and valleys, deserts and oceans, frostbite and heatstroke, action and dormancy, as well as everything in between. We are limited to all of reality because we are only a part of it and have created very little of it; our Creator holds the true perception and understanding of what really is. When we act with a belief and faith in where we have come from and only attempt to control what we realistically can influence, we experience a broadening of our reality; we begin to envision the truth that all things are possible.

We as a nation, if we are to continue through life as "One Nation under God," need to trust in our Creator and get down to the business of living in reality and experiencing the whole truth. We can only grow up stronger and more committed to one another when we learn and take on living in the present, dealing with the here and now and turning lemons into lemonade, then sharing it with everyone at a bargain price so His bounty is spread to everyone willing to accept it. In order to live life we need to experience it, all of it, and avoid the longing to escape to utopia, obsession, infatuation, or yearn for things to be constant. Life constantly changes, and to be blessed to live, breathe, and adapt in it while traveling along its highway as a community holds more treasure than any form of escapism. When we dare to live in reality with truth as our guide and love as our purpose, there is nothing on earth, short of heaven, that can compare! Furthermore, by living this way we define our own destiny as well as pave a clearer path for those who will follow.

Enron Building Houston TX

HOW MATERIALISM AND CAPITALISM HAVE CONSUMED THE CORE VALUES OF DEMOCRACY

∾

Democracy is fundamentally founded on individual rights as they relate to and benefit the community, rights that are established by the very same people they are invoked on. The core virtue that evolves from our democratic republic is the supreme power resides in the people through elected representation. We are all responsible for the fashion in which our governing public servants (elected representatives) steward the laws of the land—that allow us the freedom to pursue life, liberty, and happiness. Our community and the boundaries we set are formed from the morays and folkways with which we conduct our daily living. Our government officials act directly or indirectly for the people they have been elected to serve. They introduce proposals (H. R. Bills) on behalf of the community; then they legislate on whether to incorporate these bills into law. Next, they sign passed bills into law (Congress and the president), and finally these laws of our community are enacted and monitored through the justice system.

We the People still eminently hold the power because we are responsible for the creation and adherence to the principles we've set up to serve us. The nature of how we organize our governing bodies in terms of positions, responsibilities, term lengths, authority, fiduciary responsibility, and oaths taken form a unique check-and-balance system, a system that protects and benefits We the People, a government commenced by the people, for the people. Our freedom is predicated on how responsible we are to our civic duty and obligation. The more we understand and educate ourselves to the laws and boundaries, we as a people have established, the more freedom we afford ourselves to contribute to a better society, one that enlivens all our citizenship and dispels the threats and challenges that attempt to dissolve us as a country.

Since the early 1960s we have been transitioning from a society that manufactures and produces primarily for ourselves as well as exports goods and services to the rest of the world into a service- and consumer-oriented society that thirsts and hungers for materialism and capitalism in order to outfit our own comfortable utopia—buffered and fragmented from both internal reality and the plight of the rest of the globe. During the past two-and-a-half decades, we have immersed ourselves in the illusion that technology, materialism, and capitalism can lead us to the nirvana we've been searching for. We have strayed from the concept that these components support and provide a basis for an enhanced democracy to having these components replace our version of democracy. The foundation that has allowed these fundamental aspects to flourish at an exponential rate has given way to an ideology that touts these tangible assets to be the cornerstone of our existence. We are rapidly conceding to these economic components, letting them consume the intangible pillars that give these inert objects value in the first place. By holding materialism and capitalism as the zenith to aspire to, we have slowly bled the life and virtue out of the real valued treasures of this land, We the People.

To continually indulge our egos with the vision of having the best of everything material created through capitalism, we have expensed and taxed our soul as a united community. Our children today lack the moral principles of democracy and instead are filled with apathy because of the exploitation and marketing of materialism and capitalism as the answer to our prayers. They are being fueled with the notion that consumerism without real purpose, for status's sake and self-comfort, takes precedence over cooperation and community. They are brought up with values that foster getting to the top by possessing the biggest balance sheet and the highest net worth—disregarding who is trampled on ascending there. We place more value in what we consume and acquire than interacting, relating, and sharing these provisions with the greatest valued asset of all, our neighbor. People and their diversity hold the keys to a successful, healthy, growing America. The unity with which we tackle challenges and share the spoils becomes the real measure of our value and net worth.

Materialism, capitalism, and the advancement of technology are highly valued factors in their own right that can contribute immensely to the wealth of a democracy. It is when these factors are viewed and marketed as having more value than the structure they are contributing to—our democratic republic—that they start to consume the very core that has lead to their existence. We can't continue down this path that separates and buffers us from one another using materialism and capitalism as the end all, for this will disconnect us from relating to our fellow citizens. The adverse affect of taking the human element out of society leads to apathy with regard to caring and opens up Pandora's Box favoring manipulation over love in our relationships. Greed and rationalization replace truth and cooperation. Individualism for the enhancement of the community and diversity to expand the unity of the nation are apt to give way to personal gain and self-comfort for a few at the expense of the many. When there is no intrinsic value attached to creating massive monetary gain through raw materialism and capitalism, we drift off-course into a darkened sea that lacks a moral compass and becomes non-navigable. We lose all lifelines, and our purpose gets consumed in the oblivion we are now charted for. We lose the network that has taken years to fortify and our place in the world becomes tarnished, counterproductive to the rest of humanity.

In order for materialism and capitalism to thrive in our society, we need to view its value as complimentary to our democracy, one of many contributing and enhancing factors that pronounce the strength, resolve, and beauty of our land. These key components, when successfully integrated into our society, generate genuine value to be shared with everyone. Democracy is the cradle that houses and nurtures capitalism and materialism as well as a multitude of other tangible and intangible aspiring factors. No one component will outshine democracy, for like the organs of the body, each donates a priceless contribution to life; but separately each is not developed enough to sustain life by itself.

Once again we see opportunity for trust, responsibility, charity, citizenship, accountability, and honesty as the freedoms derived from materialism and capitalism when they are directly related to democracy. They are a force for good when proportionally melded into the fabric of our society—they assist in creating an appealing beacon for all to strive for. We need to extend this type of culture to those who wish to be a part of it, and we need to share the wealth produced to avoid becoming despondent and consumed by these individual factors that standing alone are but temporary, inert byproducts to the priceless whole.

Like the entities that produce our wealth of materialism and capitalism, if the going concern doesn't take into account all the assets and liabilities as well as the retained equity and goodwill of its people while growing and serving a purpose (if it hoards its riches unto a select few), time and circumstances will catch up with the imbalance and what was once a healthy, growing concern— producing for the community—will become reduced to a life in dire straits, struggling to carry on, in need of a lot of tender loving care. By consuming wealth at the expense of others rather than expanding wealth by investing in others, we become consumed in our own materialism and capitalism; and the democracy which embraced these once cherished components is reduced to survival of the fittest. If we promote democracy as the venue to which materialism and capitalism can create added value, then our society will become the benefactor of these enhancing properties and we can turn a dead end into a thriving roadway once again, this time bringing everyone to a higher level, for our newfound tangible riches will be imbedded in the greater intangible wealth we will acquire in our expanding democracy.

US Savings Bond

OUR PARADISE AT THE EXPENSE OF THE WORLD AND WHO WILL PAY FOR IT

⚭

The following are some major statistics that document how we, the United States, create our wealth at the expense of the rest of the world:

- We compose less than 5% of the world's population and contribute about 10% to the world's energy needs while we consume almost 25% of the world's energy resources.[xiii]

- Our national debt has ballooned from nearly five trillion dollars a decade ago to over twelve trillion dollars at the end of last year.[xiv]

- Further, our government projects over a trillion dollars per year increase to this deficit balance for the next several years; this is with inflation being held to historical lows over the last ten years.

- More serious than these statistics is our trade deficit which has been skyrocketing out of control at record pace for several decades now; this is with increasing exports during the same period of time.

- Compound this with the current high unemployment rate, the recent slide of the dollar against other world currencies, and the near zero percent return for which we are currently auctioning our Treasury Bills for (the key subsidizing component to our financial structure[xv]) and you begin to see the disastrous recipe we have concocted for ourselves.

The foundation we have been developing our nation on over these past few decades has us leveraged to the point where real change is being witnessed that is no longer within our own control. The rest of the world is waking up to the reality that we have been living in a paradise at the expense of others without sharing the wealth or investing back in their cause. How long can we expect our neighbors to subsidize our lifestyle when we continue to ignore their hopes, dreams, and visions? We are the biggest contributor to the planet's environmental concerns, and it has taken until the past few years for us to acknowledge this fact let alone start to make an effort towards working with the rest of the world to amend for our irresponsibility and generate a cleaner, more vibrant atmosphere to live in.

For decades we have been living on borrowed time and credit with our consumption fueling our economy. We have been living and promoting our paradise without regard for who is paying for it. We have deluded ourselves into thinking that we can consume our way through these struggling times and sweep our debt under the carpet or bundle it away in junk financial instruments and pawn it off on the next guy. We have lowered our guard and rationalized away our responsibility to one another and the world community at large so that we can enjoy and maintain our comfort off the backs of our neighbor.

By displaying such apathy to our neighbors and greedily taking advantage of others' misfortune while dismissing the long-term affects we have leveraged on our society, we have successfully managed to produce the sad plight we find ourselves in today. We have depleted the favorability we once secured around the globe, and as a society we have manipulated one another to the point where we cast blame on everyone and everything but ourselves. We could all use a big mirror to evaluate how each of us has contributed to the crisis we find ourselves faced with.

Our first step should not be a knee-jerk approach, nor should we institute bold legislation that will temporarily avert hardship in the short term if it will prove more costly in the long term. We should first humble ourselves to the reality and pain we are experiencing and then analyze the root causes that have led us to this point. We need to realize that it is "we" who have to pay for the grandeur we have basked in over the last quarter of a century. We must educate ourselves to the truth that there is "no free lunch" and no "bailout plan" that can alter the effect caused by the greed and selfishness practiced over these past thirty years. We have been morally bankrupt as a nation far longer than we have been monetarily bankrupt, and our first course of action should be to make amends with our immorality before attacking the economic instability we find ourselves living in.

As citizens, corporate citizens, small business owners, charitable organizations, entrepreneurs, employees, unemployed, government officials, healthy, sick, and distraught individuals, we need to see who we really are in the complexity of our society and how we contribute to shaping the environment we live in. Are we acting with the intent to furnish hope and restore goodwill to one another, or are we merely focused and only interested in padding our bottom line? Are we creating and expanding the American Dream for all our citizenship so our community shines for all people, or are we resided to working for self-interest and the enrichment of ourselves at the expense of our fellows?

To be citizens of the United States means to live as a community that meets the challenges of the day, creating opportunity, and spreading hope for liberty, with the vision of justice for all. It doesn't mean becoming perpetual opportunists concerned only with becoming independently wealthy while ignoring the needs or ambitions of others. Too many of us have gambled with the mindset of becoming wealthy so that we can live as we please, discounting that real success includes giving back and fostering vision for our neighbors so they can enjoy the pilgrimage to their success. True success promotes true paradise—where trust honesty, responsibility, and goodwill lead to hope, faith, and love. The bounty that we create incorporating these qualities into our daily living is the by product that allows us to grow and expand within our means; ultimately generating perpetual promise and light for the future.

As a nation, we must invest in our own paradise and work to the common good this democracy lends to all its citizens. There is a time and place for everything, and the time for accountability and morality is now. In order to build unity which produces abundance, we all need to face our national economic crisis with a contributing heart—we must sacrifice and commit to today in order to flourish tomorrow—and take the necessary actions that will open up opportunity for long-term growth rather than settle for a temporary fix that will only complicate our course down the line. We must resolve ourselves to the reality that this is our watch, and we must act prudently with the purpose of meeting our responsibilities so that the world gifted to us can be afforded to our children, and in turn they can pass a better tomorrow on to the next generation.

All great civilizations of the past have met their end because humans have let power corrupt and blind us to the true treasures that generate strength in the first place. When we act without giving thanks and prosper without humility—for it is through grace and mercy we are blessed to do so—we disconnect ourselves from the community and diminish its growth. If we boast in a bold and brash manner that we are superior to our brothers and sisters, we stir up negative animosity that fragments and pits one against another. We stunt our growth as a society and risk becoming another fallen civilization. We build on limited resources because our intentions are manipulative and our cause is to satisfy our own ego rather than fortify a strong community.

To perpetuate this land of manifest destiny, we must unify our spirit and work from the gratitude of having an opportunity to fulfill a purpose while sharing the fruits of that labor leveraging love as the resolve for all. We are indebted for what we garner; it is up to us to give back so that our world can be enriched by us contributing to it while living in it. Let us pare down our debt and amend our past transgressions so we can once again pursue happiness with a just cause and entice the world to the same end. To promote a healthy, enriching lifestyle we must first reconcile to one another; for it is through reconciliation that the pathway for resolution and wealth shall be opened.

RIGHTING A LISTLESS SHIP

☯

Charity, cooperation, empathy, faith, grace, hope, humility, love, reconciliation, respect, responsibility, substance, surrender, unity, and vision are some of the major resources we are in short supply of when reflecting on today's America. In order for us to live up to the principles we have evolved from, it is up to us to learn and acquire for ourselves these intangible resources that back and foster the goodwill of the tangible currency we conduct our daily living with.

It is the will of our society that needs to be tended to, first, before we move forward with infusing a monetary remedy. Life is a constant test, and buffering ourselves in haste without a thought-out plan, pumping massive debt into a reeling economy before resolving the root cause of the illness, is like taking aspirin for the pain cancer is causing; it may momentarily mask the symptom but it never attacks the systematic cause of the illness. To truly cure the current ills that plague us as a nation, we need to understand the underlying reasons why we are in this state. We need to reconcile with the reality we are in—quit casting blame, for there is enough to go around—and put into place fundamentally sound policy that produces good faith and fairness practices. We need to start building trust in one another once more so we can move forward, resolving our dilemma with a well-constructed long-term growth plan and taking responsibility for the shortfalls we have encountered. We need to enact accountability for our action and nurture a benefit for all parties involved.

Every one of us is responsible for our actions and the influence they have on our society; with our freedoms as citizens of this great land comes the responsibility to conduct our lives in a fashion that adds value to our community. If we plan on righting our ship, we will need to take ownership for both the good and bad our business places in the world. We will need to forge new trust in the days ahead that will convey empathy and contribute solutions that take into account a healing for our past and a positive attitude that lends hope to tomorrow. The anger and frustration that eats at us from the inside out will need to be replaced with innovative spirit that holds promise and substance for how we mature as a country. The leadership we elect to bring about this change will need to re-gentrify the governing process so our society renews its faith of being governed by people who commit to serving for the people. The government will have to reinforce the checks and balances established that allow this land to grow and prosper according to the will of the people. It will have to be a government that enables the people to live in freedom and to facilitate our maturity enhancing the community we all comprise.

Rationalizing that government holds the answers to our problems lacks responsibility on our part as citizens, for we all play a hand in how we steward this land. Government in a democracy is formed to assist in carrying out the passions and wishes of the people. It is a structure set up to guide and protect us as a community while we are acting with individual freedom to pursue a better life. We need to provide sound government in order to afford the freedom for our open markets to operate and generate opportunity for all. We cannot expect government to replace the private sector or take over the burdens created by manipulation and mismanagement of a few bad apples; this will limit the tree's growth and strangle the potential and vision to develop our country. What we can expect our government to work feverishly towards is a better representation and foundation for our free markets to operate in—one that promotes fairness, good faith, and establishes deterring recourse for those who choose to play outside the rules for their own gain. It must be a government that regulates in the best interest of the majority yet allows the freedom to introduce new innovative ways to produce positive prosperity for the whole society. We need to realize the village is made up of many diverse people, each offering significant value when given the opportunity to positively contribute to the community's success.

We need to get rid of the acceptance that anything goes as long as it makes "me" rich and replace it with the richness that contributing with a bigger purpose of benefitting one another will lead to making all of us wealthier. By educating each other to the understanding that true wealth carries far more value and goodwill than any monetary measure could reflect we can all experience the success of seizing and creating opportunity that benefits and enriches more than just our generation. We will have used our resources and time wisely, leading our nation to new heights and addressing and serving the world's needs. By bearing our daily crosses and utilizing the gifts we have been bestowed, we will avoid the temptations that civilizations past have bowed to and lead by serving, acting, and displaying the true sense of purpose we were originally established for. We will again welcome our tired, poor, huddled masses and together travel to a new mountaintop creating immeasurable wealth that will eminently reflect the power of our soul—in God we trust.

Let us define our course, morally heal ourselves, and then in unison with sacrifice take the steps needed to refine the American Dream to include quality for all who place country and neighbor ahead of self-fulfillment. The road to everlasting riches is not measured by what we acquire throughout a lifetime but rather by the wisdom we impart having lived a full life. We need to convey to our inheritors that investing wealth will create a better world for all. We need to teach each other how to fish for the morrow rather than catch fish to supplement today. [xvi]

When we as a society can reconcile to one another for the benefit of creating a robust tomorrow, when we can all see that taking on our individual responsibilities leads to increasing the abundance we have been blessed with, we will be enlightened as a better community that stays lit through love and burns with eternal hope while extending faith through caring for each other. Our strength resonates in our cause, our confidence comes from believing that success is failure turned inside out, and our endurance comes from committing to each other—gifting with the gifts we have been given.

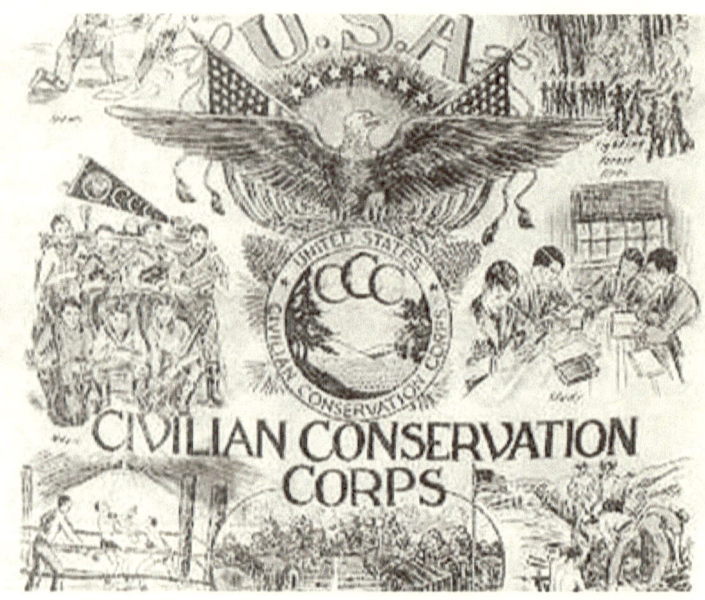

Civilian Conservation Corps Camps in Michigan

DRAFT FOR COMMUNITY SERVICE

Much like the old Armed Services draft and in the venue of the Peace Corps or the American Corps, we need to organize a Community Draft that networks high school, college, and postgraduate personnel to utilize their knowledge and gain valuable work experience while rebuilding the infrastructure of our communities. This program should retrofit our roadways, electrical grids, waterways, bridges, tunnels, public buildings, railways, sewer systems, and various other systems that relate to and affect the general public. The major impact of such a program would compare to the New Deal, more specifically, the Tennessee Valley Public Works project FDR instituted to take on several of our nation's challenges that were dragging our country down during his tenure as commander and chief. If set up in affiliation with our higher learning institutions (including state and county colleges) we could invest in a proving grounds environment that would allow our youth the opportunity to gain valuable employment as well as pare down their debt, congruently outfitting a very much in need infrastructure with state-of-the-art design and technology for optimum public utilization. We would be attacking our unemployment situation, addressing significant public need, providing invaluable work experience to our future leaders, and expanding opportunity into adjacent private sectors of the economy.

By preparing a force to meet tomorrow's issues, we could also expand the services and provide assistance to developing countries, burrowing into our trade deficit on a new front. We would also be promoting to the world a peace-building initiative that revitalizes our unity with our neighbors on the planet but doesn't impose an ideology on those countries. This type of program would go a long way in restoring our tattered relations around the world without having to be the lone ranger or policeman of the globe.

A commitment by citizens willing to take on and take advantage of a promising situation for all, set up in similar fashion to how the service academies are presently run—bartering education for service commitment—would combat the debt today's youth are strapped with when entering the workforce from school. By contracting for a certain period of time, this new work force would be far more prepared and command more consideration coming out of this program with a proven track record, entering the private sector. Another benefit would be to our major institutions that are forecasting a huge shortfall in the engineering field over the next decade. Instead of hiring from offshore, we would be able to employ US talent that has gained fruitful experience both at home and abroad.

Instead of pumping loans into Fannie Mae and Freddie Mac, why don't we lend money directly to citizens who will benefit from utilizing the investment, being incentive driven rather than debt ridden? Again, this would show accountability, responsibility, and citizenship enhancing the entire community, in turn resurrecting us as a thriving, expanding nation once more. By investing in ourselves this way, we will gain the confidence to dream a brighter future with real substance rather than saddling ourselves with insurmountable debt and less authority and autonomy for decades to come. By taking the time to plan, structure, implement, and regulate a program of this stature, we would be reestablishing many of the core values that led to our abundance shortly after World War Two.

Sometimes it becomes wiser to slow down and take baby steps in order to analyze and digest the predicament we find ourselves in, then make educated decisions that foster long-term value, digging out of a ditch instead of extending the rut. This type of action and measure will cause tremendous sacrifice and commitment; but the return of investing in a Community Draft program far exceeds the risk of borrowing mass amounts of funding just to stabilize a badly managed economy that shows no real up side absent of a major overhaul. This type ingenuity coincides with the heritage we have evolved from. By investing in ourselves and utilizing our potential to create a brighter world, we will have given our future a fighting chance; and this opportunity will be backed by our sincere faith and goodwill strong enough to lead us all to a better place. Let us slow down a bit so we can evaluate all our options before rashly limiting ourselves to mediocrity for an indefinite period of time.

In lieu of putting our future in harm's way, let us take harm's way out of the picture by offering peace through service to those willing to accept it; the guaranteed allegiance we forge with the rest of the world will captivate enough strength and resolve to contend with those who resist and harden their hearts for the sake of their egos. The intensions of our service will be to better humanity and our ability to extend talent and fortune to those in need, to accept diversity and its leveraged value so that freedom and opportunity proliferate and the beauty of its merit can be shared by all. We are part of a melting pot culture, a nation that exemplifies the wealth housed in working with one another to provide a better way for all who seek to be a part of something bigger than ourselves. By displaying a unity at home, we will entice others to pursue similar passions, and we will all be better for it. Let us take the log out of our own eye that blinds us from realizing the potential that could be and begin to renew a trust within our society that strengthens and shines a light bright enough to guide the way.

If we are going to borrow and place debt on ourselves, why not disperse it in the form of an investment directly to those who will be paying it off (We the People)? As mentioned before, it is better to teach someone how to succeed than reward them temporary success. By outfitting our future work force with tools and skills to provide for themselves, we will give them opportunity for independence. If we only borrow to bail ourselves out today, we limit any long-term growth and will leave ourselves farther behind when today turns into yesterday. A draft for community service would give us a leg up on reversing a situation that has been years in the making. In addition it would bring much needed promise and spawn a new attitude and optimism. We owe it to our past; we need to pay it in the present and invest it in our future. What I am speaking of is the American Spirit.

NATIONALIZING AND REGULATING ESSENTIAL VITAL INDUSTRIES THAT SERVICE ALL AMERICANS

Currently, one out of every nine working US citizens is considered a government employee. Whether it is at the local, state, or federal level, this equates to over 11 percent of our work force collecting a paycheck from Uncle Sam.[xvii] When people balk at the mention of nationalizing or regulating an industry, they fail to realize that our current way of commerce is not so far removed from this scenario. Vital industries that affect the general public on a daily basis and transcend socioeconomic barriers need to be addressed and structured from operating in open markets to being regulated or nationalized. When the average citizen is adversely affected during his or her daily living by the way economic commerce is conducted in a specific industry—when open markets cater and show bias to a certain class for the sake of profit—we breech the rights we have established under our Constitution to provide equal opportunity under the law.

Certain industries such as transportation, health care, energy, communications, and the financial sector affect the entire social and economic stratosphere. The people that are affected by these industries are citizens of our community and as such have certain fundamental rights in need of protection from inequality produced by unfair competition in our open markets. In order to foster equal opportunity, fair trade and good faith need to be enforced so the public does not become a victim of unfair competition.

Herein lays the conflict to having totally free markets verses socialism. In our democratic republic, we need to distinguish needs from wants, then apply the right environment for an industry to operate in so the majority of the public is yielded the benefits of that industry. In other words, the playing field needs to be leveled and made just, in order to promote optimum operation. If competition creates fairness by driving down cost, at the same time providing quality and reasonable access, then everyone stands to gain from this environment. It is when free trade produces gross imbalance due to influence and bias within a vital industry, affecting the lifestyle of all our citizenship, that regulation and/or nationalization must be entertained. We need to structure the industry to allow all those participating equal opportunity to benefit from its existence. Whether it be nationalizing or regulating a particular sector, we need to create an environment that entices quality, affordability, value, and wealth to all participating parties including management, employees, customers, vendors, taxpayers, regulators, and everyone else who is affected by such commerce. Only those industries that have a vital impact on the way we conduct business and live on a daily basis should be structured in a manner that invokes the rights and freedoms of our citizenship. Be it nationalizing or regulating, checks and balances ought to be mandated. Periodic review and reconciliation to policy and procedure need be applied by independent organization to secure and grow the goodwill and vibrancy within the business sector.

All Americans deserve the right to health (health care), to travel about the land (transportation), to communicate with one another (communications), to stay warm in the winter and cool in the summer (energy), and to save and invest with the security that fair trade and lending provide when practiced in good faith (financial). Citizens need protection and security from being taken advantage of when it comes to providing the vital necessities we should all be endowed with. There needs to be a trust built within all our industries (nationalized, regulated, and open) that guards citizens from fraud, waste, and abuse. With safeguards in place, optimum operation of nationalized and regulated industries in the context of our overall economy will foster fair competition in the open markets. A high degree of confidence ascertained in these nationalized and regulated industries will complement our open markets, making for a thriving commerce that produces positive influence in the world. The reasoning for considering these options is that they will provide protection to the citizens where free competition may be viewed as a liability rather than an asset. We weigh the benefits to the entire community against the restrictions placed on the industry itself, and where there is net gain we should move forward in the best interest of our society.

A case in point where regulating or nationalizing an industry would be in our best interest can be witnessed in the energy sector of our economy. When gas prices skyrocketed over the past few years from an average of $1.25 per gallon to $4.00 per gallon, who reaped the most benefit (during the first eight quarters of this price increase, oil companies pulled in larger revenue than what was recorded as GNP for over 90 percent of the world's countries) and who suffered the most (citizens and transportation dependent businesses had to reprioritize their budgets and felt severe negative impact during the same time frame)? Our overall economy has suffered greatly due to the way we have let commerce in the open market manage our energy needs, steering us into a dependency relationship on foreign oil for the sake of short-term gain. With a major focus on generating a huge windfall for their shareholders, a select few, these "publically" held companies have leveraged the welfare of our entire nation for the sake of lining their own pockets. They have gotten caught up in the greed and control of comforting their constituency at the expense of the general population—albeit mainly within the legalities of free market trade.

If we regulated or even better nationalized major portions of the energy sector for the stability and welfare of our people, we would open up opportunity within this field to generate avenues leading to independently providing for our energy needs. In addition we would create more exports of alternative, renewable energy to productively assist other countries with their energy concerns. We would be able to concentrate on living and relating to one another with virtuous value, real assets that this country could use and share to expand our goodwill to more of humanity. We would be able to commit more resources to competing in free markets at home and abroad, bringing prosperity back to our community while enhancing the environment of our neighbors.

Nationalizing and regulating certain key industries so we can compete in others for the betterment of our country may be viewed as socialism by some; I prefer to look at it as the next chapter in the American Dream. By stabilizing vital components that affect the welfare and commerce of our entire nation, we leverage our ability to compete and broaden the opportunities to pursue life, liberty, and happiness in today's world. We continue to paint a masterpiece on the canvas our forefathers established, developing new dimensions that enhance the beauty of our portrait and attract the value of those who seek to be renowned artists in their own right.

RE-GENTRIFYING AMERICA: BUILDING TOMORROW'S INDUSTRIES AROUND SOLVING TODAY'S PROBLEMS

∾

Ask not what your country can do for you, but what you can do for your country.

—John Fitzgerald Kennedy

An individual has not begun to live until he can rise above the narrow horizons of his particular individualistic concerns to the broader concerns of all humanity....What are you doing for others?

—Martin Luther King

The spirit fills us, God is ready; but we must be the ones to take action. The service we engage in and provide to others is how we take on challenges and brighten the world around us. We are faced with heavy burdens in our country today, and if we give in to the greed, neglect, apathy, and rationalization that has pushed us in this direction we will always view the challenge as insurmountable. But when we take on hope as an attitude (Honoring Our Principles Eternally—Happiness Of Presently Existing—Harvesting Our Personal Experience—Helping Others Pursue Eternity) and draw together as a community to face our weaknesses, as a nation we transform our spirit to take positive action to resolve the present-day dilemmas and grow our ability to turn our visions into reality.

By humbling ourselves to our inequities and taking steps to overcome adversity, we begin to face our challenges without fear. We develop the confidence to plan, make intelligent decisions, and commence action to heal and right an ailing, listless nation that has been fragmented for far too long. We have been blinded by fear and division, and our development as a community has been paralyzed by individual greed and complacency. We have momentarily lost our way due to our diluted ideals, thinking we can manipulate our community for the sake of individual gain. We have hidden behind a Red State, Blue State mentality and rationalized that one way is the only way.

In doing so we are missing the message that value and leverage created in the diversity within our United States is where our real prosperity resides. We have shortchanged ourselves because we have caved in to the temptations of greed and selfishness. We have ceased living by the command, "Do unto others as you would have them do unto you,"[xviii] disregarding the consequences of our actions and neglecting to account for all the value in our community. We misuse the gifts of technology, manipulating its advantages for self-gain and comfort while diminishing the human impact, effects we are casting on our neighbors. Technology in its own right has neither a positive nor a negative influence on humanity; it is how we as humans choose to implement technology into our society that adds or detracts value to our environment.

We are living in transitioning times where concepts of "change" and "opportunity" are taking on new meaning. As a nation we are at a crossroad where we will be making major decisions that will hopefully unite this land and re-gentrify our conviction to serve one another, building new trust. This trust will forge a renewed confidence, sparking the flame that will once again ignite a new prosperity. This trust will take into account the whole community when resolving the challenges of our day. We will not fit all the pieces to the puzzle simultaneously; but we can unite in our attitude to find common ground for moving forward in our action to complete the picture.

A major step once again transpired with the peaceful transformation of power that took place in our capital in January of 2009; our new government conveyed empowerment back to We the People. A clear message of hope and unity is attempting to make its way past the economic, environmental, wartime crisis into the mainstream fabric of our society. We are beginning to envision a new morality based on the historical pillars that have grounded this great land from its inception. We are once again trying to build a bridge to tomorrow that embraces the lessons learned from the past; we place our country and everything good that she stands for ahead of personal gain. We are renewing the enlightenment seen by our forefathers—"we are the change that we wish to see in the world today."[xix] The strength of our citizenship to reign in freedom is harnessed not in competing against one another; rather it emanates through the devotion of being responsible to and for one another so that as a community we believe that all things are possible. This promotion of unity and community are the healing steps that will lead us from division, despair, frustration, fragmentation, gluttony, and greed to the development of humility, inclusion, justice, kindness, love, mutuality, need, promise, reconciliation, success, trust, unity, vision, wealth, expansion, yield, and zeal. Then we can account, build, capitalize, delight, enrich, fight, and grow a maturity that forgives our trespasses against one another and leads us to develop relationships with one another to go forth and witness a better way.

The reality of creating this new trust will build confidence and character because it will be founded on our belief in one another—in the good we humans have to offer—rather than on inert material that in the absence of our better nature becomes the dividing temptation that diminishes our purpose and pits us against one another. In order to use the bounty we are blessed with to create life, liberty, and happiness, we need to empower our souls with the freedoms and responsibilities that bring out our compassion and will to provide a better society ahead of fulfilling self-gain. By taking on the bigger cause of comforting our neighbor, we will be rewarded with more comfort than we could ever imagine. Achieving this goal as a community will open the way for turning the challenges of our economy, environment, health care, education, and social concerns into opportunities for growth, expansion, renewal, and enlightenment. We will once again invest in each other instead of adding debt at the expense of one another. The wealth we obtain as a sum will far outweigh the actual sum of the parts. Our goodwill will be measured in the service we give and the appreciation with which we act; it will be the standard that backs our value rather than an overextended credit that keeps us afloat.

In order to move forward and reverse the depressed state we are heading towards, we will have to become innovative problem solvers attacking several issues of concern congruently. By planning broad initiatives that address an array of challenges, we can serve to several fronts with wisely invested resources. Resources when implemented will tend to our immediate needs and when fully vested will generate greater abundance for our future development. If we stop focusing on bottom lines and instant returns from the investment we apply and start concentrating on creating healthy concerns with solid products and services, we will provide for long-term growth. We will start living in the present achieving this growth.

We can start this re-gentrification on two fronts right from the start. First, we can trust and support the leaders we elect, backing their decisions to initiate plans that disclose the root cause of our challenges and then take steps to resolve them with continual dialogue and action including all parties (every branch of government as well as the people they govern). We citizens must live up to our responsibilities to the community by educating ourselves and being the checks and balances to those we entrust to serve us. By acting together and working to a common cause we all stand to benefit in re-gentrifying our nation.

Secondly, we can take individual action in our everyday living that will impact our society now and into the future. Before acting impulsively for immediate or short-term comfort, we should reflect a moment whether our actions will solely benefit "me"; will they infringe on others and will I be enriched enough to add value to the whole by embarking on this experience? Am I acting on a feeling or are my actions going to fulfill and create a better environment? In other words, will I be yielding a benefit for long-term growth or will my action consume and perish without regard to the community I live in?

When we become more conscientious regarding our environment and the affects we have on it—be it running several errands in one planned trip, replacing candescent light bulbs with energy-efficient ones, recycling our trash, investing in quality, community minded entities, volunteering in our free time, donating to worthy causes, going out of our way to assist a neighbor, living a healthy lifestyle—we begin to take responsibility in our action, and this opens our lives to more freedom. We also become role models for one another and learn how to enrich our community by relating and getting involved with one another. By standing up and accounting for our everyday living, we learn to nurture our diversity and grow a healthier community that elicits unity rather than uniformity—our talents find opportunities that allow us to grow individually while respecting the attributes of others, and together we cultivate a better way of life for the entire nation.

To think that we won't constantly be challenged with existing and new concerns would be foolish and unrealistic; but if we stop challenging ourselves to make life in our country better for all, we won't stand a chance at carrying this experiment to the next level. Our dreams of today and the possibilities for the future will cease to exist, and we as a people won't come to fruition.

To re-gentrify America we need to reinvent our infrastructure (utilities, roadways, major urban and suburban planning and development, and communications) as well as where and how we acquire our energy (go-green alternatives as well as conservatism). In addition we need to restructure and regulate our financial institutions in order to promote investment from within and abroad. Our government needs to provide the tools and foundation for fair and equitable trading—to create positive goodwill and stability which in turn will generate trust and confidence to those willing and wanting to succeed in these markets. We must reestablish financial markets that operate and reflect true value to those who invest in them as well as to those who custodian the investments. To open these markets to prosperity once more, we must reeducate the players to what the definition of prosperity is. We cannot measure success solely focusing on instant return; we need to broaden the analysis to include long-term growth and stability, tangible and intangible gain. The value for investing must take into account the direct and indirect benefits that underwriting such promising potential lends to the total market. We need to look past the unprecedented gains and losses produced from speculation, sensationalism, and irrational volatility, and ground our vision of success in a secure and longer lasting environment.

To fuel the markets with resources and without regard for long-term growth and stability is to prolong the transaction from illness to health by masking the symptoms but never attacking the cause for a cure. We need to nurse our sickness by educating, discovering, and enacting sound principles that will build growth and prosperity on fundamentals that have fortitude and commitment at the core of their soul. We cannot drift with the tide and build on sandy ground in order to smooth over the rough spots. If we don't disclose and reconcile our current habits, we run the risk of drowning in our efforts to surface back to a mirage. We need to protect ourselves from ourselves because we are our own worst enemy.

When we gain from coercion, deceit, manipulation, preying on others' weaknesses, we unleash our darker side, which leads to selfish greed, apathy, and discontent; it disconnects us from one another. When we think in terms of win-lose, we set ourselves up for failure; we don't give ourselves the opportunity to grow and succeed, and we walk through life with a distorted perception of the truth. We hold our opinions as fact and our world becomes limited because of our rush to judgment and inability to witness reality. Contrary to this, when we work towards making a new success formula or plan by combining the beneficial aspects of all the parties involved, we build on solid ground reconciling to the past, understanding the present, and gentrifying the future.

Re-gentrifying America will take an awaking of all citizens to the realization that we as a nation must leverage our diversity, understand and work with each other to forgive and heal our society. We must invest in one another to afford ourselves a better tomorrow. Success is failure turned inside out, and it gets defined by people of character who are willing to give more than they receive. We are measured collectively by how we treat one another individually, and our ideology will only resonate in this world if we have the courage to act on our beliefs without regard for personal gain and for the benefit of all.

America is defined by our history, and throughout all this history our defining moments have come out of our darkest, weakest hours. The real beauty we portray is the perpetual hope we convey in the midst of our lowest days: that despite our human shortcomings we acknowledge God's grace to our country and attempt to extend the same to one another. So our experiment lives on. We are not always right in the action we take, but our intent is always to do right in creating liberty and justice for all.

Piece of torn down Berlin Wall in garden of Reagan
Memorial Library, California

FIGHTING TERRORISM WITH EDUCATION AND NONVIOLENCE

Going to war should be the last option we resort to when all other alternatives have been exhausted and when there is a clear and present danger to our national security. The War on Terror has been around since Cain slew Abel, and we have sadly compromised our leverage against this evil by preemptively going to war with Iraq under false pretense. Further, we have compromised relations with our allies by this change in ideology. By initiating conflict—all for self-gain and retribution—against a potential threat without regard to or direction for liberating a society that didn't request our aid, we have diminished our goodwill in the world; we have suffered, and our history has been given a blow, another dark chapter of the ugly American.

We have tried to fight terrorism with sheer brawn and ignorance, relying on our independent military might rather than attacking this mentality and mechanism of warfare with education, collaboration, and diplomacy. By acting so brashly and unilaterally, we have been perceived as the enemy we are struggling to rid this planet of, and we have compromised the ideals that give us strength. To fight violence with violence only begets violence, and no one becomes the better for it. If we conceive that we will be the victor because we will have stamped out terror, we are naïve and are rationalizing success in the midst of failure. No one wins when we go to war against each other because we are all gifted life from above—we are His creation and as such, what right do we have to extinguish His gift? Do we not become the terror we wish to eliminate from the world? This perception depends on whose eyes it is emanating from. If we truly wish to vanquish terror from our lives, don't we first need to address that the temptation will always exist to terrorize, as long as humans inhabit this planet?

This nation has been founded on the freedom to live and prosper responsibly with each other in peace—respecting each other's beliefs and cultures, honoring the rights to life, liberty, and the pursuit of happiness. And after every major war, we have implemented to some degree this same promise when rebuilding and restoring these fallen nations. Our vested interest has been to restore humanity to living and growing in peace with one another. Why is it then that we approach terrorism with the mindset of fighting fire with fire? Would not we be better served and united in our cause with the rest of the free world if we served those terrorized with support through education, diplomacy, understanding, and resources to combat and dismantle terrorism? By limiting the threat, holding it in check, and exploiting the limitations of its use, wouldn't we strengthen our resolve with all those who face terrorism by acting jointly to deter this evil in life? Is not the use of diplomacy and conviction to peace a stronger weapon to thwart the impulsive, destructive acts of violence and corruption that constitute terrorism? Won't we vanquish this enemy and free people from its grip by teaching that its use limits and controls without yielding any fruit? Shouldn't we combat this disease (terror) by exposing its one dimensionality, an insatiable quest for control?

Terrorism, like cancer, focuses on a weak link of a healthy cell to create a new, mutated cell. This dysfunctional cell has similar properties to an ordinary cell— except for conscience and humility. Without conscience and humility, the mutation perceives itself to be better than the organism it resides in and tries to gain total control by expediting reproduction; it seeks to replace and eradicate the origin from which it evolved. Failing to see the grace that allowed its fruition and dismissing the need to relate to and enhance its environment, essential ingredients for sustained growth, the cancer ends up consuming itself because it lacks the capacity to give. Terrorism by its very nature ends up the same way cancer does; in the end it is self-defeating because it can't survive on its own and it contributes no lasting value to humanity. If we can define the concept of terrorism to those being manipulated by it as well as to those using it without resorting to violence in conveying this message, we would be implementing our greatest defense against this disease and enlightening the world to a better way of reconciling and resolving our differences.

If we stand true to our beliefs and tout peace, education, respect, understanding, and empathy over terrorism, violence, chaos, and control, we will empower the artillery of community and civility to defend against terrorism. Our strength will come from fostering love and acceptance, remaining true to our convictions and sharing the peace we've achieved while growing our society. We will again place war as a last resort to be used only when our society is threatened with extinction. Terrorism will have no fear to feed off of or prey upon. We will show our might by displaying our capability of defending our rights and what is rightfully ours, but defer using it when education, diplomacy, wisdom, and other nonviolent means can be our primary weapons of deterring terrorism. By promoting peaceful ways of defending ourselves, we will endure and make the world a better place for all who wish to live and love in the freedom of their sovereignty while relating and respecting the lifestyles of others. With nonviolence we will open up the world to a new degree of civil diversity that entices good over evil and diminishes the vain effort of terrorism to take center stage. Terrorists will soon realize the limitation of their ways and have no recourse but to give way to the abundance of love that transcends every culture and frees us all from our sins.

As we continue to understand and educate people in our country and around the world to the sanctity of life, sharing the good life brings to one another, we implement a stronger defense than any nuclear, biochemical, or conventional weapon ever could. Our hearts, souls, and spirit contain the real ammunition for the battles against terrorism. The atrocities we commit against one another proliferate because as humans we rationalize and disconnect our relations when faced with the truth that there is good and evil in all of us. We are all capable of terrorizing one another if we choose to embrace selfishness, greed, power, control, and any other concept that places us above humanity. This temptation has been around since the beginning of time. It is when we surrender to the good that reigns within us, to view all of humanity as one, that we gain insight into our best interest and the strength to carry that will into action.

Sacrifice for freedom's sake means taking responsibility to protect and defend liberty's cause even at the cost of our own life. To take an offensive posture against terrorism using war as a first line of defense is to become terroristic in its own nature.

We erode the good intentions for struggling with this conflict in the first place; we may beat back terrorism, but at what cost? How will we look upon ourselves when the conquest is over? Will we have changed our principles from the encounter? And can we overcome the contempt that flares up in our hearts, having acted in the same manner as those vanquished? There are no winners in war; everyone becomes a casualty to some degree.

War and violence are sometimes unavoidable when defending the values and virtues of our land. When we decide to go to war, we need to be united, agreeing that this is our best course of action and the reasoning for this decision will be justified as a result of the conflict. We must be able to accept our differences and build towards a peaceful future once the smoke clears. And we should go to war only if we can be true to our convictions and build new relations, reconciling our past and working toward a civil future. Having learned from our inequities, maybe we can mature to the day when we can all begin to live with the opportunity to seek life, liberty, and happiness, accepting our differences and applauding the higher common ground we have broken in the quest to live and serve for each other. Our best weapon against terrorism is not force; it is to educate and live in unity as one race—a diversified race called the human race—acknowledging the differences endowed by our Creator and living His will rather than our own.

CHALLENGING TODAY'S YOUTH TO DREAM AND VISION A BETTER TOMORROW

☙❧

We learn from our past and plan for our future, but we can only live and make a difference in the present.[xx] America is known throughout the world as one of the richest nations on earth, yet we find ourselves lacking in education and falling further in debt with ourselves and those who invest in us. We are squandering vast resources in pursuit of immediate gratification, blind to the definition of true wealth. What promise are we extending to our children if the loftiest values we aspire to are merely material in nature? Why have we used our children, sending them on their way with a mountain of debt, to seek our own comfort instead of teaching real value and character so that tomorrow's leaders can serve with tools and skills that will make a real difference?

We must challenge today's youth to dream a better tomorrow by gifting them with the knowledge and ideals that will truly allow them to make an impact with their contributions. We must awaken their consciences to the talents, passions, and ability they possess and guide them with love, support, protection, hope, promise, and faith so they can harness their worth and confidently make a real difference in tomorrow's world. We must change the present climate of fear, debt, limited opportunity, stress, and tension and replace it with incentive, openness, adventure, affordability, promise, and growth. We must give our children the opportunity to succeed and the faith to follow their dreams. We need to reconcile our own outstanding issues so there are fewer burdens placed on our heirs, and more wisdom to nurture them. We need to start acting prudently in order to bequeath value that enables our youth the possibility of fashioning their American Dream.

The stewardship we convey today will be tomorrow's history that our future will have to learn and grow from. Wouldn't we be fulfilling our service to our children by reflecting some discipline and value in our lifetime that instills a guide for them to venture into the world with? Shouldn't we focus on gifting them a moral compass and the tools that will allow them to contribute to a brighter future rather than saddling them with debt and competition they are ill equipped to handle?

How can we continue to bankrupt our future for the comfort of today? Materialism, greed, and selfishness have caught up to the goodwill we inherited from our parents. For too many years we have abused a trust that's been passed down through the generations of this great land, and now is the time to end the "me" generation and start living the "we" generation once more. In order for the American Dream to persist, we must endow our youth with the realization that dreams do come true if you live with humility, grace, and appreciate the goodwill and support you inherit.

Thomas Merton said, "No man is an island."[xxi] To achieve our American Dream, many have invested in our happiness. We are indebted to those who have paved the way to our better day; now is the time to repay the favor to tomorrow's dreamers so their aspirations can be fulfilled and lead them to higher heights while simultaneously opening up opportunity for others to share in the wealth. "We are all born with a purpose no matter the circumstances surrounding our birth."[xxii] It is up to us to blaze a trail that fuels and taps the potential we carry within.

To live the American Dream, as opposed to reaching for individual wealth and aspiring to personal desires, constitutes a common theme of thanksgiving when those dreams take on reality. The true essence of living the American Dream can be found in the manifestation of sharing opportunity with others rather than in the comfort and satisfaction of achieving our own goals; we are appreciative of the success afforded to us, but our focus must ascend to leveraging that success to others. By gifting back, we challenge those in receipt to fulfill their own promise and pass the torch on so all living in our society who seek a better life can afford to. Pleasure then comes through giving rather than receiving, and investing rather than consuming becomes our purpose.

As we challenge our youth to work towards a better tomorrow, let us meet our challenge of today so that a new independence infinite in hope and prosperity replace our finite realities of debt and dependency. Let us gift the strength of interdependence and community rather than the separation of greed and selfishness. To live out a dream means to build relationships and share a trust with one another. Further, it means contributing to the success of others and sharing in their dreams as well. As we grow up, the wisdom we acquire through life's experiences fills us with the confidence and courage to embrace our diversity and unite for a greater common cause, sharing and investing in one another's lives, acting in faith, and trusting our beneficiaries will wisely use the resources inherited to pursue their purpose in life.

If we believe in this land of manifest destiny and teach our children well, they will overcome the challenge of their day, brighten the torch of freedom, and lead by serving the rest of humanity a chance to fulfill their dreams and aspirations. Together we will raise new generations to the place where God created and intended us to be, custodians of His eternal kingdom—a land where all are created equal and endowed with the unalienable rights to life, liberty, and the pursuit of happiness. We will garner our strength in the opportunity we create from the challenges we meet, and the peace and prosperity we proclaim will be shared for all to gain. There will be mountains to climb and valleys to cross, but if we trek along as one, we will fathom enough love to conquer any inequity standing in our way.

We must embrace all our community to join in this pilgrimage for united we stand, divided we fall. In our time let us mend our ways, seeking grace from each other and giving mercy to those who sincerely wish to reconcile. Let us pare down our own burdens through hard work, wise investing, and disciplined spending so that when the time comes for today's youth to take on tomorrow's problems they can act and operate from true wealth governed from lessons learned. Let us give them the hope as well as the incentive to dream a brighter tomorrow, one that fulfills their purpose and expectations and carries us all to a higher concern. If we teach our children to steward with reverence, they in turn will guide the future with the same core values that God blessed this land with when we declared our independence back in 1776.

I want my country back not for my own concern as an individual but so our children can understand the sacrifice that's been laid down before our time to get us to this point. So that they will realize that dreams only come true if we commit to achieving them with all our heart, mind, body, and soul. Setbacks will be inevitable and daunting challenges will creep in. Some of our days will be filled with darkness, and at times life will overwhelm us; we need only have the patience to look where we have come from, staying persistent to our cause. If we are flexible with our spirit, firm with our resolve, supported in the grace of our Creator, and accompanied by our fellow human beings, we can form a new reality that captures our American Dream then gifts it to all those who are called to our light. The service with which we ascend to our goals will determine the climate in which this country grows and will form the community that will inherit our legacy.

We have been blessed to live in this land during our lifetime, and it is the responsibility of the whole flock to tend to each other. Living united, we will reap the great harvest, share with all our bounty, and cultivate a wealthier orchard that will bear fruit for all who hunger. With freedom comes the opportunity to understand true happiness and in appreciation offer that understanding to those who wish to walk along its path. The dawn is coming, and a new day will shine forth granting us the chance to form a better partnership among ourselves in the hope that building trust in our community will open up greater opportunity for the future. We have been tested before and will be tested again; if we draw from our strength of unity and on the talents and blessings we have acquired, there will be no challenge too great or insurmountable.

We have been promised that if we remain true to ourselves we will be gifted grace from above. The light that shines upon this land will guide us to answer God's calling and not our own. God has blessed us, and if we will be true to Him by being true with each other, His love for us will reign brighter and brighter.

EPILOGUE

We have become lost in the shuffle of chaos that has led us into a turbulent sea of challenges on all fronts and accounts. With the world shrinking and continual demand to expedite larger and faster, we are escalating ourselves into oblivion and leaving insurmountable debt for our children to live and aspire from. How can we feel comfortable knowing we have placed our future under such leverage and with such little promise?

The challenge for us in today's world is to find stability and consistency backed by accountability, integrity, and a high degree of confidence. The federal government has got to redefine what it should actually be undertaking in our society today. Should we be looking for a one-stop shop in the government, or should we be looking for a moderator, an enforcer that sets the boundaries of the playing field and backs those laws without becoming an active player or just another principle within the competing landscape? Without segregation of duties and an adequate check-and-balance system to provide fairness for our citizenry, we run the risk of bankrupting our governing goodwill as well as the trust built up in our country over the past two centuries.

Do we really want our government to take on all the inequity in our society by integrating into every avenue of the economy, or do we want our government to house the structure and enforce the regulations that our markets are willing to participate in? Wouldn't the government have greater leverage and sounder clout if it focused on regulating and promoting good faith rather than become fully vested in the challenges we've created by ignoring fairness, honesty, and justice in the first place? By positioning ourselves as principle stakeholders (taxpayers funding the government) in every major industry that is ailing, we have Band-aided a dire situation and compounded the risk of restoring stability and growth through open markets. We are leveraging our future right off the map because the debt we are taking on is not what we owe ourselves; it is what we will owe to the countries that own us! Before too long these countries will be pulling the purse strings and setting policy that determines how we live as a society. Our freedom to govern ourselves will become a thing of the past!

Let's not be so hasty to pump such huge amounts of borrowed funds into our economy just for the sake of jump-starting a condition that has been brewing out of control for decades. As stewards to and for each other, let's get real to the fact that the gravy train has run dry and we have not gotten wiser in the wake of the reality facing us now. Let's educate one another to the real reality we are presented with and calm our panic with the reassurance that over a reasonable period of time and everybody contributing, we will right this economic ship, giving the society of this great land healthier opportunity to become wealthier having navigated through difficult straights as a community. We need to change the mentality of our country and steer it away from becoming a purely material, capitalistic, comfort-dependent culture towards a stable, moral, community-based, and intangibly driven society—one that deals with its problems today, taking action that resolves our dilemmas today, and offers hope, faith, wisdom, and opportunity for tomorrow instead of more debt and dependency, which ultimately will change the value and visions of what once was a promise land.

Our children need hope, incentive, promise, and love in order to keep the freedom America stands for alive. It isn't about the almighty dollar anymore; it is about the trust that this medium in commerce once stood for and the goodwill that people backed it up with. The value is created by how we relate to one another, not by how much currency we administer. We the People need to fully understand both the benefits and liabilities we are redefining our economy with. We need to turn the corner from being reactionary to the present economic situation and start taking smart, well-conceived initiative that has vision, incentive, and growth built into a long-term path. This kind of action will raise the whole country's esteem, values, and quality of life: a total wealth package with an emphasis on intangible qualities rather than a monetary fix that concentrates only on the tangible and leaves our goodwill depleted.

Until we address, understand, and reconcile the root cause of our economic crisis—which in reality is a moral crisis—no amount of stimulus or bailout money will restore or prevent this landslide from reoccurring. When analysts convey that the markets need to have confidence restored before the wheels of commerce begin to roll again, I don't think we understand the full impact of what they are espousing. When a crisis of confidence occurs at the magnitude we are seeing today, a real breach of trust has transpired to cause this effect (all across the board). Trust is needed to move forward and grow relationships, and it can only become solidified over time with a track record. When broken, we can forgive expediently because forgiveness deals with the past. The past cannot be relived; what is done is history.

Again, I state that trust is at the heart of the matter because our economy is fostered, nurtured, and grows on relationships. These relationships are forged over time by pledging commitment, hard work, quality standards, and good faith; and then, acting on every component mentioned to assure satisfaction is guaranteed with the deliverable. Further, that consideration is well received by all parties involved and there is mutual benefit on all sides. This is how confidence, honesty, integrity, promise, quality, responsibility, and trust work their way into our economy and create growth and tangible prosperity (a byproduct of acting in good faith).

This is what America was once recognized for and has fallen away from. No quick fix is going to right our ship overnight; at this point anyone with realistic expectations and faith in this country to heal and proceed in a healthy way has resided and committed to a long-term turn- around. Every one of us has a role in creating a new trust with ourselves as well as with the rest of the world. We are part of a bigger picture, and if we're going to endure and be a contributing factor we need to realistically take and account for meaningful actions that will once again lead us to the freedom we profess and long for.

A transparent society that grows and thrives on freedoms and relationships that enable the fabric of our country to truly resonate the values from which we have been founded on; a country that shines and radiates healthy growth, equality, liberty, justice, faith, vision, and the way to a brighter future—this is the country I want back for my children and their children. The stewardship with which we live today can only reflect the love we have inherited and the value we wish to pass on. If we are true to one another in our action and in our character, if we place the higher cause of sharing our wealth with our neighbors above comfort for ourselves, we will be well on the road to recovery. Our souls will transcend this mortality, and we will have conveyed our Creator's love in the miraculous fashion He intended when He gifted us life to do so. God bless the land I love and all the inhabitants that glorify her. God bless America!

REFERENCES

Brother Lawrence. *The Practice of the Presence of God: Conversations and Letters of Brother Lawrence*, Oneworld Publications, 2009.

Carlson, Richard. *Don't Sweat the Small Stuff—and It's All Small Stuff*, New York: Hyperion, 1996.

Carnegie, Dale. *How to Stop Worrying and Start Living*, Pocket Books, 2004.

Covey, Stephen R. *The 8th Habit: From Effectiveness to Greatness*, Running Press, 2006.

Hartdegen, Stephen J. *The New American Bible*, Canada: World Catholic Press, 1987.

Mapp, Alf J. *The Faiths of Our Fathers: What America's Founders Really Believed*, New York Oxford: Rowman and Littlefield Publishers, Inc., 2005.

Morgan, Edmund S. *The Birth of the Republic 1763—89* 3rd edition, Chicago: The University of Chicago Press, 1992.

Tolle, Eckhart. *A New Earth: Awakening to Your Life's Purpose*, Plume, 2006.

Warren, Rick. *The Purpose Driven Life: What on Earth Am I Here For*, Michigan: Zondervan, 2002.

NOTES

i Mahatma Gandhi, 1869–1948

ii *The 8th Habit,* Stephen R. Covey, 2006

iii "Made to Last Forever," *The Purpose Driven Life:What on Earth Am I Here For?* Rick Warren, 2002.

iv "The Discovery of Inner Space," *A New Earth: Awakening to Your Life's Purpose,* Eckhart Tolle, 2006.

v "Peggy Conlon—CEO and President, The Ad Council," *In The Face of Uncertainty: 25 Leaders Speak out on Challenge, Change, and the Future of American Business,* Martha I. Finney, 2002.

vi "...that all men are created equal and should be endowed with certain unalienable rights which include the right to liberty, justice, and the pursuit of happiness"—"The Declaration of Independence," *The Birth of a Republic 1763-89: Third Edition,* Edmund S. Morgan, 1992.

vii Luke 10:29-36,The New American Bible, Stephen J. Hartdegen O.F.M., S.S.I., 1991.

viii *One Nation under God:An Anthology for Americans*, Robert Gordon Smith, 1961.

ix Newsletter US Visa March 12, 2006, New York, New York," USA Greencard Center.

x "We need to listen with our hearts, think with our minds, and act with our bodies guided by the spirit that protects all men from their limitation and humbles us to the grace and mercy we seek and long for every day of our mortal lives."—Stephen R. Covey, 2006.

xi   *Tilting at Windmills: History and Meaning of a Proverbial Allusion to Cervantes' Don Quixote,* Wolfgang Mieder, 2006.

xii   *How to Stop Worrying and Start Living,* Dale Carnegie, 1987.

xiii US Energy Information Administration: Independent Statistics and Analysis 2008.

xiv "Our national debt has ballooned from nearly 5 trillion dollars a decade ago to over 12 trillion dollars at the end of last year."—The Daily History of Debt Results, Debt Held by the Public and Intergovernmental Holdings, www. TreasuryDirect.com, 2009.

xv   *Capitalism Unleashed: Finance, Globalization and Welfare;* Andrew Glyn, 2006.

xvi Luke 5:1-11, The New American Bible, Stephen J. Hartdegen O.F.M., S.S.I., 1991.

xvii US Bureau of Labor Statistics 2009.

xviii Exodus 20:1-17 (The Ten Commandments), The New American Bible, Stephen J. Hartdegen O.F.M., S.S.I., 1991.

xix Mahatma Gandhi, 1869–1948.

xx   Church Bulletin, Sacred Heart Riverton, NJ, 2010.

xxi *No Man is an Island*, Thomas Merton, 1986.

xxii "You Are Not an Accident," *The Purpose Driven Life: What on Earth Am I Here For?* Rick Warren, 2002.

www.ingramcontent.com/pod-product-compliance
Lightning Source LLC
Chambersburg PA
CBHW020442290526
45785CB00002B/979

* 9 7 8 1 4 5 3 6 7 7 9 9 5 *